W9-CIZ-579

Needlepoint
Made Easy

"And though our country everywhere is filld
   With ladies, and with gentlewoman, skilld
   In this rare art, yet here we may discerne
   Some things to teach them if they list to learn."

JOHN TAYLOR

From *The Hand-Book of Needlework,* by Miss Lambert,
published New York, 1842

*the text of this book is printed
on 100% recycled paper*

Needlepoint
Made Easy

Classic and Modern

by
MARY BROOKS PICKEN
and
DORIS WHITE

Drawings and Layout by CLAIRE VALENTINE

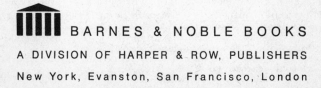
BARNES & NOBLE BOOKS

A DIVISION OF HARPER & ROW, PUBLISHERS

New York, Evanston, San Francisco, London

This book is published in hardcover by Harper & Row, Publishers, Inc. It is here reprinted by arrangement.

NEEDLEPOINT MADE EASY. Copyright © 1955 by Mary Brooks Picken. All rights reserved. Printed in the United States of America. No part of this book may be used or reproduced in any manner without permission except in the case of brief quotations embodied in critical articles and reviews. For information address Harper & Row, Publishers, Inc., 10 East 53d Street, New York, N.Y. 10022. Published simultaneously in Canada by Fitzhenry & Whiteside Limited, Toronto.

First BARNES & NOBLE BOOKS edition published 1974.

STANDARD BOOK NUMBER: 06–463398–5

This book is dedicated

to all of you who know how to make

the beautiful needlepoint stitches,

and who have been kind enough

to take time to say to us,

"Do you know how to do it this way?"

We have learned from you

and have written this book for you

to show our appreciation.

Contents

Introduction

WHEN A BOOK IS WRITTEN to give pleasure and benefit to the owner an introduction, perhaps, is not necessary because the pages need no explanation, no amplification. Yet we want to visit with you about this book, and anticipate for you, if you will allow us, some of the pleasure that can be yours through the years when you are an expert needlepointer.

You do not have to play millions of scales to gain the rhythm, as in learning to play the piano. You do not have to practice, practice, practice, as in some professional work. You do not have to puzzle out intricate designs or instructions. You need not strain your eyes in the least, because needlepoint has been completely simplified for you in this book, as you will see as you leaf through the pages.

Learn the stitches from Claire Valentine's A B C drawings. A child can learn from them. Make a dozen stitches as shown, and you are off to success with the piece of your choice.

It is our experience that if you do a dozen rows of stitches in a piece, you will enjoy needlepointing so much that you will want to do it at every possible opportunity. That is why we suggest that you have a carrying bag so that you can take your needlepoint with you. While you pay a call or wait for an appointment, you can make progress with your stitches.

Some women say, "But I don't want to hurry the doing of needlepoint, because the work is so pleasurable." We do not suggest that you hurry, but we do want you to realize how easy needlepoint is, how completely fascinating, and how, *when* you have made exquisite pieces for your own home, you will ever be ready with the "blue ribbon" piece for the important wedding, birthday or Christmas gift.

Needlepoint is not a luxury, nor is it an extravagance. It makes sense and saves pennies and is ever satisfying. You are sure to find it so.

We, the authors, are deeply indebted to Helen Disbrow for her sketches; to Charles Palmer for art assistance to Claire Valentine;

and to Paula Bolli for detail work; to Joe Shulim for many lovely photographs. Also to the Heirloom Needlework Guild and Columbia Minerva Yarn Company, the *Notion and Novelty Review* magazine for some detail photographs. To Marcel Vertès for allowing us to use some of his beautiful designs and the story about his interest in needlepoint. Our thanks also to Dr. Peter Goldstoff and Mr. Robert Ellis for loaning us their own needlepoint pieces for photographing in this book.

Our thanks to the members of the Baldwin, Long Island, High School Adult Needlepoint Class. They kindly loaned us their prize needlepoint pieces for inclusion in this book.

THE AUTHORS

What Is Needlepoint?

TODAY'S NEEDLEPOINT has come to us from the historical tapestries of ages ago. It has served its purpose all along the way to record the art of the period, the taste and the times. The long life and beauty of needlepoint appeal to peoples of all nations.

Needlepoint is embroidery on canvas. There are many stitches, some favored over others. We give in this book those that have stood the test of centuries and the ones that are favored the world around.

Needlepoint has many stitches:

Petit point, for tiniest stitches, makes faces, flowers, and figures. With the petit point stitch, a design can be worked out as carefully as with an artist's brush.

Gros point makes the background that sets off a beautiful piece of petit point. Gros point is also used for the design in many instances. Some feel that it is a little easier to fill around a gros point design than around a petit point. Either is easy when you know how, and this book will show you how.

Gros point can be executed in several ways: continental, basket weave, diagonal, regular half-cross and simplified half-cross, to name only the most often used stitches. Master these stitches, plus petit point, and you will really know needlepoint.

Needlepoint a Mystery Hobby?

MANY PEOPLE KNOW ABOUT NEEDLEPOINT. That is, they have seen it but, because they do not know how it is made, they consider it really a mystery. Needlepoint is the simplest form of embroidery worked on canvas using a blunt needle with yarn or floss. It is easy to do and most rewarding.

Everyone knows what knitting and crocheting are, but some do not know what needlepoint is and confuse it with hoop embroidery. Many people have to be persuaded to investigate before they can realize that needlepoint is a pleasurable hobby— as relaxing as are knitting and crocheting, and equally satisfying in results.

Once you make a needlepoint stitch and see how simple it is, it will no longer be a mystery to you, but rather a compensating art, one that you can explore and benefit by in many ways.

Another mystery to many is the design, which has been hand-worked, ready for you to fill in the background. One person in a thousand will undertake to create the design itself.

Most needlepointers prefer to buy the design which has been worked by experts who have the patience to thread the needle so many hundreds of times, and skill to blend the multitude of colors to achieve a beautiful result.

With the design ready made for you, all you need do is fill in the background with a color that is right for your use of the piece. Certainly no mystery about any of this.

No, it is not monotonous to fill in a background. Rather, the rhythm of the stitches weaves a spell for you that makes the work fascinating, therapeutic and inspiring.

If You Are a Beginner

WITH THE BEAUTIFUL DESIGNS already worked—ready for you to fill in the background—you can have exquisite needlepoint, and all as easy as can be. You need not hesitate to buy a beautiful piece.

If you can hold a needle you can do needlepoint. Blind people work pieces beautifully. Children do prize pieces. So can you. It is easy to learn, and practice makes perfect. Do a few stitches or a whole row on the outside edge of your canvas "just to get your hand in," before you begin actually working your piece.

Go to your best art needlework department. See the lovely designs that are available. Tell the salesperson that you would like a piece for a chair, a cushion, doorstop or fashion accessory. Choose a piece that in design and color is right for you.

Buy a background yarn that is suitable. The salesperson will tell you how many skeins you will need. Make friends with this salesperson. She can help you in many ways. Return to her if there is a question this book does not answer.

Buy a package of size 18 or 19 blunt gros point needles and a package of size 22 or 24 petit point needles. Usually there are three needles to a package. (When a piece of needlepoint is finished, put your needles away carefully to have them ready for your next piece.)

When you get home, provide yourself with a small pair of scissors and a thimble. It is a good idea to have a bottle cork to push the sharp points of your scissors in when you are not needle-pointing.

Beginners knit or crochet with coarser yarns on a simple article until they learn, and so it is with needlepoint. Select a piece of needlepoint made on the regular ten-mesh-to-the-inch canvas with a gros point center.

If you have a chair, bench or cushion you would like to recover, practice the stitch recommended for your purpose outside the outlined area until you make the stitch easily. The first inch of stitches you make on a furniture piece will be turned under (see marking directions). After working that inch all the way on one side or end of your canvas, you will have acquired the desirable tension and even stitches that make needlepoint easy to do and good to look at.

Save the finer white canvas (sixteen squares to the inch) such as is used for wallets, eyeglass cases, pictures and such until you have mastered the regular canvas (ten squares to the inch). Then the smaller mesh will be easy for you.

Marking Directions. With chalk and pencil mark off the space where you will place your stitches—usually one inch beyond the

Gros Point Design

size of the object to be covered, if making a furniture covering. Make this one-inch allowance on all sides as you will lose a little in size by shrinkage when you block your piece, and you must have enough stitches to be sure all edges are well covered.

Make or Buy a Bag Especially for Holding Your Needlepoint. Keep your work in this fabric bag or a small box, something good-looking enough to have around so that you can pick up your work readily and do a row or two while you visit or listen. This is the happy way to do needlepoint. We believe the work will appeal so much that you will pick it up at every opportunity.

Petit Point Design

If You Are Experienced

MANY WOMEN do magnificent needlepoint. They always have a piece in progress, for their home, as a gift for someone near and dear, or possibly for exhibition. When this book comes into an expert's hands, we hope that as she leafs through, she will find some pointers that will make the book interesting and worth while. We hope that some points will be new to all of you and therefore help you to enjoy your work all the more.

Help someone you know to enjoy this work. Buy her a piece as a gift or help her select a piece. Show her how to start, using the stitch right for her piece. Let her have some of the same pleasure you have known. A needlepoint design, with possibly a known right color background yarn and needles, makes a perfect gift for the girl with a hope chest, or for a grandmother who has leisure, or a child who needs to be amused.

For experts. Maybe you aren't aware of the fact that the method you now use for working your beautiful needlepoint, while delightful to the eye when completed, is not always as easily done as it might be.

Many of you turn your needlepoint. Turning has been recommended for centuries as one of the ways to work. Try working your various needlepoint stitches only one way, without turning. As no time is wasted trying to keep the point of the needle from catching into the yarn in the previously worked row, greater speed is achieved. The needle goes down into the bottom corner of the stitch and rarely catches the yarn, thus eliminating the uneven ridge that sometimes detracts from a smooth, even finish.

Maybe you are not starting your needlepoint piece in the right spot. For example, many of us have started our needlepoint pieces, using the continental stitch, in the lower right corner of the canvas, making it necessary to put the subsequent row above a previously worked row. This is the same principle as turning—you work against the yarn (often catching it) rather than inserting the needle down into the previously completed row.

Experiment with these ideas with an open mind and then continue with the method most enjoyable for you.

Do Needlepoint for Pleasure

WE HAVE SAID that needlepoint is relaxing. It is the rhythm, the uniformity of the stitch that soothes. It takes a little while, maybe three to five minutes to develop the evenness, the even pull on the yarn so all stitches are the same size. Try it on the edge of your canvas if you haven't been doing needlepoint for a while. Establish the rhythm before you actually start work on your piece, so that your stitches will be uniform and not too tight.

Good quality needlepoint canvas is strong and sturdy, so you need not be gentle with it. Stretch it, roll it, crumple it. It will take much abuse. Plan to take your needlepoint with you wherever you go because on a train, plane, or while visiting, you can get many beautiful stitches made and will lose the feeling of being tense or in a hurry.

When Buying Needlepoint

WHEN BUYING NEEDLEPOINT remember this. Needlepoint fits in—you can use it with classic (period) or modern décor. Choose the design and color that appeal to you and that are right in scale as well as color for the object and the room. This way—whether your room needs designs that are dainty, severe, formal or bold—choose that which is completely right for your purpose.

The good art needlework department has hundreds of pieces of needlepoint in petit point and gros point designs from which you can make a selection. You should be able to find in stock designs suitable for chairs, stools, benches, rugs, screens, accessories and religious subjects. If you have something in mind, it is a good idea to tell the salesperson of the department what you want. The chances are she will be able to find something in the department's stock that will be completely appropriate to your need.

Large stores hold frequent sales of needlepoint. This is not distress merchandise. Sometimes new patterns are coming in from the manufacturer and the stores need to make room for the new in their inventory; or they were able to make a special purchase and offer you good prices.

8

But don't think ever that needlepoint is expensive—because you get so much in return for any purchase. Regardless of the initial cost of a piece, if needlepoint is for furniture covering it is one of the least expensive of all upholstery fabrics because it seldom needs to be replaced and endures from one generation to the other.

Many who do needlepoint say that they benefit so much from the actual working of a piece that they have had full value from the initial investment even if they never used the piece—but they always do!

When shopping, if you see a piece of needlepoint that you think would delight someone, buy it as a gift—birthday, Christmas or wedding. But whatever you do, don't work it. Rather let the person to whom you give it have this pleasure. You may choose color of yarn to be used, but do let the recipient have the pleasure of making the piece. Needlepoint pieces such as door-stops, pictures and cushions, especially those with gros point centers, are ideal to give to children. It keeps them occupied and they can have the fun of making a gift for mother or grand-mother. Children generally delight in this kind of work and needlepoint will keep them occupied for hours on end.

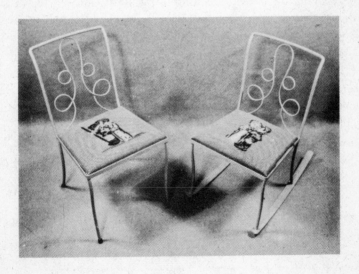

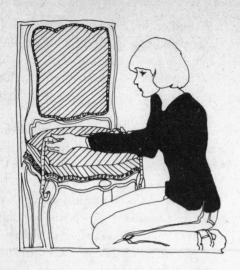

How to Measure an Object for Needlepoint

For Furniture. Measure the surface to be covered from edge to edge, measuring both the depth and the width. Use a tape measure for this and be accurate. Allow one inch all around on all four sides for turning in when mounting. For slip-seat type furniture allow at least two inches on all four sides. Measure the top of the object, then make your allowances on all four sides. Mark with pencil on the canvas. On the finish line use double basting thread, going over the pencil line with uneven basting stitches. This basted line in our book is called the "outlined area."

For Pictures, Cushions and Fashion Accessories. Work at least two meshes beyond the actual area to provide a seam or turn as the item requires.

The Size of Your Canvas

BE SURE YOU BUY CANVAS large enough to allow sufficient material for mounting on your piece of furniture. Whatever you make has to be attached to something, and there should be at least two inches of unworked canvas plus one inch of worked canvas on all sides to attach to the object.

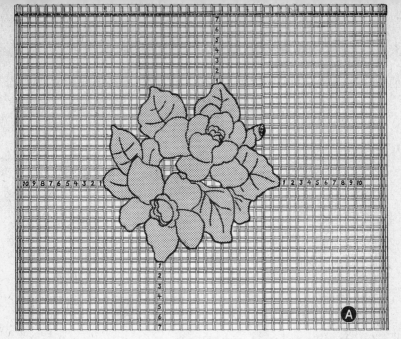

Designs are not always in exact center of the canvas. Before you have marked the area to be worked, count the large meshes right and left of the design. You must have an equal number of meshes on each side, and an equal number of meshes top and bottom. See diagram **A**.

Counting and making sure your design is centered are important in every piece you make, doubly so in accessories such as belts, wallets and bags.

The Size of the Needlepoint Design

THE PATTERN SELECTED should be in proportion to the size of the object to be covered. A small chair needs a small design; a large, heavy chair, a large design.

Often one-quarter of the canvas is filled by the design. Excepting for repeat and all-over patterns, *at least* one inch of background area should be allowed to show beyond the extreme edges of the design. Floral sprays and bordered designs should be centered, leaving at least one to three inches of background area visible around the design. All-over and repeat patterns should cover the entire surface.

11

How to Determine the Amount of Yarn
for Needlepoint Canvas

FIRST, MEASURE SURFACE to be covered from edge to edge of a slip-seat chair. You need two full inches of canvas on each side and both ends for turning.

Choose a canvas with precise clear meshes. The regularity and evenness of the meshes help to insure smooth, even stitches. The obvious distinction between large and small meshes also makes working needlepoint "easy on the eyes."

THE QUANTITY OF YARN NEEDED:
(For double mesh—10 meshes per 1 inch of canvas)

The Continental Stitch. Multiply length of canvas by width (area to be covered). Approximately 1¼ yards of needlepoint wool is required to fill in 1 square inch of canvas, so multiply by 1¼.

Example: Area to be covered—20 inches x 20 inches = 400 square inches

Multiply 400 by 1¼ = 500 yards of wool needed

If a 40-yard skein is used:
Divide 500 by 40 = 12½ to 13 skeins

If a 100-yard skein is used:
Divide 500 by 100 = 5 skeins

The Regular or Simplified Half-Cross Stitch. Same formula as above—multiplying by 1 in substitution for 1¼. (Approximately 1 yard of needlepoint wool will fill in 1 square inch of canvas.)

The Petit Point Stitch. Same as for continental stitch except four-ply needlepoint wool should be parted in half.

The Diagonal Stitch. Requires approximately the same amount of yarn as the continental stitch.

The Basket Weave. Requires approximately 1¾ yards of yarn for each square inch, or a generous one-third more than the continental.

Essential Materials for Needlepoint

CHOOSE A PIECE of needlepoint that you want to make. Have at hand a size 18 or 19 and size 22 or 24 needle. (The size 18 or 19 is used for the gros point and size 22 or 24, for the petit point stitches.)

If you sew, and you use a thimble, by all means use it for needlepoint. If you do not use a thimble, try to learn to use one because it does speed the work.

Keep at hand an accurate tape measure for measuring a chair or stool when you want to buy a cover for it.

Have a pair of small sharp-pointed scissors for snipping the yarn. Keep a cork at hand to put the points of the scissors in to protect the points and to make them safer for you.

A lead pencil and a piece of chalk are also desirable equipment for marking the working area of the canvas before basting.

Needlepoint Wool (often referred to as yarn). Needlepoint wool is 100 per cent virgin wool made expressly for needlepoint of long, strong fibers which do not fuzz easily. The dye qualities, the mothproofing plus long-wearing quality are desirable for needlepoint. Knitting or crocheting yarns are not recommended for needlepoint as they are made up of shorter, softer fibers and will tend to fray as they are being worked.

After cutting a skein of yarn, as shown on page 18, locate the knot and snip it off—so it is out of your way.

Needlepoint Floss (Embroidery Floss). Mercerized cotton or in rare cases silk floss is used to work the finer white canvas. Eight-strand floss is recommended to properly fill in this canvas. Most floss is six strands; therefore, it is necessary to add two strands from another length. The remaining four strands can be used double in your needle.

Any unfinished edges of canvas bind with bias binding or twilled tape so the canvas will not fray or tangle with your yarn. This also insures a firm edge for blocking.

Needlepoint Canvas

WHEN NEEDLEPOINT was first developed, all the materials used had to be made by the individual, and one of the materials people had to make, before they could even begin the first stitch, was the canvas. They used a loosely woven fabric, similar to our unimesh canvas, which as the name implies is a single mesh. It didn't have stiffness and consequently the meshes would tend to close while working. If each thread wasn't carefully counted as each stitch was made, it was fatal to the design.

There is no doubt that needlepointers of the past would marvel at our present-day canvas. It wasn't until about 1865 that a French artisan invented our modern double-mesh canvas which clearly separates the meshes, assuring perfect stitches. The canvas we use has been treated to give it a semistiffness, adding body to the piece and preventing the threads closing.

Usually when buying needlepoint people are concerned only with the design, but it is a good idea to hold the canvas up to the light. If the meshes are not even, the spaces clear, and if you cannot see large and small meshes, it would be better not to buy that canvas because evenness in weave is essential. It tangles your yarn less, makes for quicker work, and gives a better result.

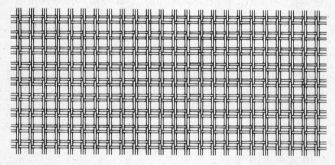

Cotton canvas is made of all qualities, sizes and widths, and is manufactured in England, France, Germany and China. French canvas has been in favor since 1865 and is considered a stand-by. However, other canvases have been developed that are considered completely satisfactory.

To sum up: when buying canvas, look for the greater regularity and clearness of its threads, and, above all, the squareness of its meshes—an object of very considerable importance to the needlewoman, whose work might otherwise become distorted by the design being lengthened one way, and shortened the other.

In this connection, a good canvas—because of its regularity—is good for the eyes rather than a strain, as each stitch is easy to take and thus helps to encourage a rhythm of work that is desirable exercise.

Elsewhere we say that needlepoint is relaxing; that it really weaves a spell in its own right and makes you not only eager to do it but reluctant to put the work down, once you are at it. Good quality canvas is a factor in this very desirable therapeutic result.

Which Is Top and Which Is Bottom of a Piece?

YOUR CANVAS has alternating large and small meshes. The two vertical threads in your double-mesh canvas are always locked together, as our diagrams show.

Horizontal threads are separated more than the vertical threads, as you see. The selvages indicate the sides; hems are at top and bottom.

Study the design in the center and you will notice how the stitches are made. Make your stitches to slant in the same direction as those in the center design, whether they are petit point or gros point.

If you look closely, you will readily see which is top and which is bottom of a piece.

As explained elsewhere, begin regular half-cross at the upper left-hand corner. See detailed stitch instructions.

Begin your simplified half-cross stitches and diagonal stitch at the lower right-hand corner; continental stitch and basket weave at the upper right-hand corner—and just the reverse if you are left-handed.

Usually the name of the manufacturer or distributor is printed on the bottom of a piece.

Don't concern yourself too much if there are stitch flaws in your first piece. Blocking and steaming do wonders in concealing imperfections.

Needlepoint Basics

TO DO NEEDLEPOINT all that is necessary are: two needles, canvas, yarn, thimble, pencil and a pair of scissors. But you add certain things as you work: a container for your work; this book for reference; graph paper for mottoes, borders and initials; clippings and magazine articles about needlepoint that may encourage you to undertake more elaborate pieces than you have done before. And a variety of pieces to work on, to sustain your interest.

More important than all but the actual essentials is the knowledge of the stitches themselves, so that you can begin work on any piece any time with assurance.

Once you master the fundamentals of needlepoint, this art is forever yours.

Learn to Read and Follow Instructions

WITH YOUR NEEDLEPOINT WORK in your hand and a threaded needle, begin each stitch as directed, concentrate as you read, and do exactly as told. The first stitch, then another, and another will form as you work, and you will see how easy needlepoint is to do. You would not make a cake and leave out eggs, baking powder or sugar. You must follow instructions for a good cake; and so with needlepoint. Master it for complete success and enjoyment.

You must *read, look, see,* and know what you are doing and then "away you go," making beautiful stitches almost without looking. Needlepoint is the most intriguing of all handwork and you will be reluctant to put it down once you learn to do it perfectly, because it holds you always. You think, "I'll do just one more needleful of yarn," and on and on until first thing you know your piece is finished.

In this book we have tried to give the instructions in such a way that you will feel we are right beside you, pointing the way.

We want you to use this book as reference if any question arises. We hope you will become expert enough to teach others so that they too may enjoy this pastime.

Cutting Yarn

A 40-yard skein. Cut through all loops at one end of the skein. Strands are now even.

B Leaving the label on for a neat holder, pull each strand out of skein as needed.

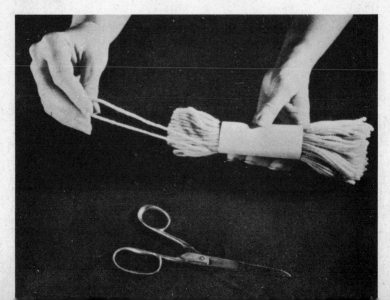

C 100-yard skein. Remove the yarn from the label and open it out so that you have a long loop. Cut the skein through, then divide the yarn into thirds lengthwise. To do this, fold in three and cut on the fold. This gives you the recommended short lengths right for working. Make a loose knot in each of the three units of yarn so you can draw a length of yarn out as needed.

What Is Worked Wool?

WOOL THAT IS PULLED through too many times looks *worked* in a row. It is not as rounded, tends to thin, and sometimes shows the canvas. This is a big reason in favor of the shorter needlefuls of yarn. You work your yarn less and consequently have more uniform stitches.

Since you are actually weaving your yarn in and out of the canvas, even the very best yarn will in time thin out and look worked. Avoid this by always using the shorter length in your needle.

Don't end every row of yarn in the same place. Alternate even if you have to stop when a needleful is half used. You can use the short length in your needle to fill in around your design.

Threading the Needle

A For easy threading, use the needle as a bridge, drop three inches of wool across it, and hold in place with your finger.

B This creates a small yarn loop which should be pinched tautly between thumb and forefinger close to the eye of the needle.

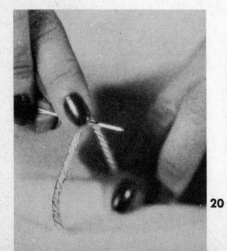

C Withdraw the needle, leaving the small loop of yarn flattened firmly between your fingers.

D Then set the eye of the needle over the small loop and relax the pinch, forcing wool gently through eye (yarn up into eye—not eye down on yarn).

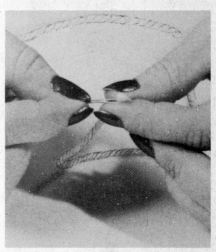

E Pull doubled yarn through eye of needle. Works every time. Easy on the eyes, the yarn and the disposition.

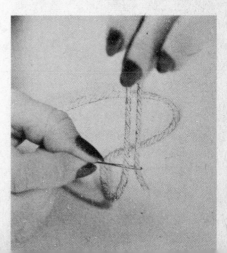

Locking the Yarn on Your Needle

THREAD YOUR NEEDLE, draw the needle down about four inches, slip it through the yarn two inches below the end. Draw the long end of the yarn to the right to lock the yarn securely in your needle. This saves needle slipping off yarn as you work, prevents your using last inch or so which wears thin from constant pulling through canvas and tends to leave meshes poorly covered on right side whenever end of yarn is reached.

Caution: If yarn breaks where locked on needle (eye may be sharp) discontinue locking but never have more than two or three inches of yarn through needle. Constant pulling of doubled-over yarn through canvas creates thin stitches in completed work.

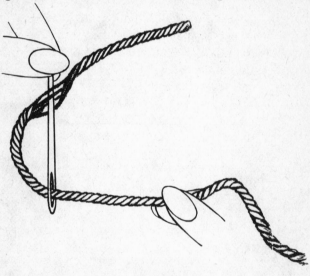

Don't Jerk Your Yarn

WE COULD SAY, "Don't pull your yarn"—not startling enough for you to remember. To get the therapeutic value of needlepoint work, learn at the outset to draw the yarn through easily, pleasurably, avoiding *jerking*. It is hard on your wool, hard on you, and tightens your stitches too much. Cultivate an easy draw and never *jerk* your yarn.

When Using Dark Colors

DARK COLORS have a tendency to be less "lofty," i.e. fluffy, than light colors. This is because of the greater weight of the dye. It is good, if you can, to pull your stitches less tightly. This is especially important to remember in doing the half-cross. You want enough yarn to cover your mesh.

If, by any chance, you find a thin place in a needleful of yarn, work to the thin spot and then cut your thread and begin anew with a new needleful. Once in a hundred needlefuls you may find a thin place in the yarn, and it is better to cut it away than to have it in your canvas. This precaution is given simply for your protection.

When doing needlepoint, no matter what kind of stitch you are using, after making the first stitch, drop the needle, allow the yarn to untwist and then begin work again. If you have twirled or rolled the needle forward in your fingers as you work, the yarn should be in a limp, relaxed position.

When You Work One Way on a Canvas

YES, WORKING ALL STITCHES in one direction on a canvas may cause it to get out of line, but the piece can be straightened quickly through careful blocking. Have no concern about this.

Putting your needle down against a previous row will not damage the yarn in that row, but bringing it from under against the row may catch in the yarn, thus retarding your stitch and fraying your yarn. Test and you will find the work is quicker when needle is put down against the wool, from the right side for every stitch. Also, if your yarn is caught by the needle as it is drawn from the wrong side of the canvas, a ridge is apt to appear on the right side which will detract from the uniformity so greatly desired.

Needlepointing with Wool

WHAT IS THE PROPER WAY to start and finish with wool? Do not use knots when starting or finishing (except in the first stitch of basket weave). Knots cause bumps to appear on the finished work and may eventually work through to the surface.

To begin, thread your needle. Make a running stitch beginning about 5 large meshes outside the working area. See stitch diagrams.

This leaves the edge flat and no ridge is formed. When ending a row, again make 5 running stitches in the mesh outside the working area, same as starting stitch.

When end of wool is reached in the middle of the row, bring it through to the back of the piece. Place the needle under the stitch opposite to the row you are working, pick up on your needle every other stitch in this row—for 3 stitches. Pull through and cut the wool off within one-eighth inch of work. Do not leave ends any longer than this because they may work through to the right side. Also, get into the habit of cutting threads off to within one-eighth inch. See detail photographs on pages 26 and 27.

To start a new needleful of wool, weave it in and out on the wrong side of the row on which you are working, beginning 5 stitches down and picking up 3 double meshes on your needle. Place the needle under the fifth stitch back from where you left off, and draw thread under every other worked stitch, bringing needle up to right side of canvas in first unworked gros point mesh, next to where you made last stitch.

Should You Work One Way, or Back and Forth? For most professional results, it is considered best to work in one direction. For instance, when working the continental stitch, which is always started from the upper right-hand corner, make running stitch to start, work across entire row, end with running stitch on left outer edge, cut thread, and begin again at right side of canvas. Some workers insist that they prefer yarn double length. However, the shorter length does not wear and become thin, and requires less "pull-through" time.

Continue in this manner, working from right to left, until you reach the design, then work down right side in toward the design, beginning at the right-hand side of the canvas for each row.

Always work the row right up to the outer edge of the design.

For filling in area on left side of design, using continental stitch, work from the design toward outer edge, and thus complete area on left side of canvas. To start thread, weave under stitches already worked in design, and end with running stitch on left side. When design area is completed, go back to right side of canvas, make running stitch and work right across the entire row at bottom of design. Continue to the marked lower edge.

For small areas around the design, we recommend turning the needlepoint, as it wouldn't be practical to finish off such short rows. In such small areas, it is easy to avoid splitting the wool in previous row by being very careful; but as suggested, it is preferred that you work in one direction for long rows because a ridge or unevenness may result unless great care is taken when turning a piece.

Starting and Ending New Strand of Yarn

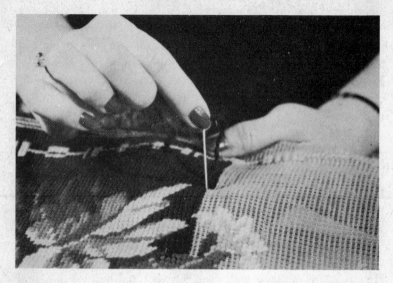

A For a smooth ending, insert the needle 1 mesh to right in the last row you finished.

B Roll the canvas and turn it over, then draw yarn under every other stitch in working row to have 3 or 4 stitches on your needle.

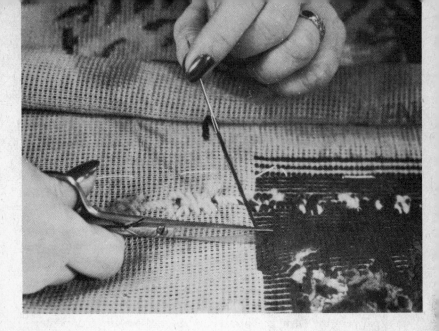

C Clip it shorter than a poodle—this keeps the back neat and flat. Avoid overlapping when you end a strand.

D To start a new strand run under every other stitch for 10 meshes opposite to the previous ending. This system insures a smooth finished appearance.

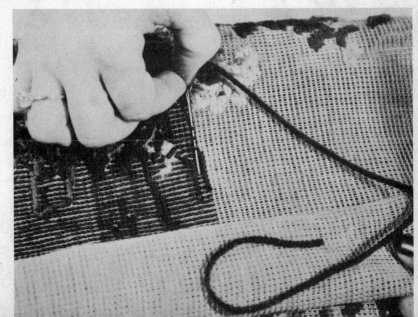

Filling in Around a Design

FOLLOW THE NATURAL ANGLE of the stitches that are in the design.

Do gros point around a petit point design as far as there are two canvas threads each way to allow for the gros point stitch. Also, use gros point stitch in closed portions of petit point design.

Petit point is more painstaking than gros point, and the stitches must be used to cover the single threads around the design. When you do the stitches correctly, they will be inconspicuous.

When filling in around a gros point design, use, of course, gros point stitches. Just make sure they slant the same as those in your design.

Petit Point Center. Gros point background should be worked as close to the outer edge of the design as possible, also in the open spaces in the designs. This to emphasize the petit point center.

Needlepoint Pieces Get Out of Shape
in the Working

WE HAVE EXPLAINED ELSEWHERE that needlepoint has a habit of getting out of shape through the process of working. Have no concern about this because if you read carefully the blocking instructions on page 64, you will see how very quickly your piece of needlepoint will come into line and be exactly true when blocked our way. A few people we have heard about have stopped work on a piece when it became, as they said, "lopsided." This is not a matter for concern because it will all straighten out completely in the stretching and blocking.

Out-of-Shape Needlepoint. Notice that this piece is not straight. The continental stitch has a tendency to make the piece slanting or "lopsided" as you work. Have no concern about this, as it will block into shape easily.

How to Hold Needlepoint Work

LEARN AT THE OUTSET to roll your canvas as you work. Roll from the bottom up and from the top down, as shown in photograph below. This keeps your canvas out of your way as you work, and this way you will never have more in the roll than your free hand can hold easily.

When using the continental stitch, working from the top down on the canvas, you can roll the worked part. Pin the ends of this roll with large safety pins to keep the finished work out of your way.

With the simplified half-cross you roll from the bottom up to the center, and from the top down to the center.

Left-handed workers roll their work opposite to the above.

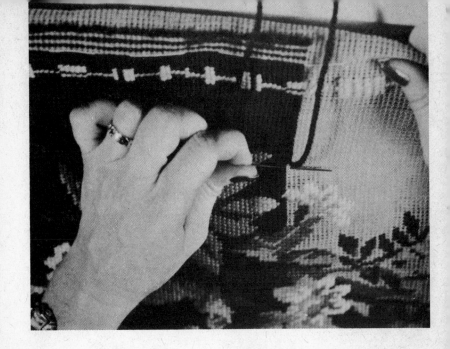

If You Are Left-Handed

A LEFT-HANDED PERSON should turn each stitch diagram (except the regular half cross) upside down while learning the various needlepoint stitches. The needle will then be in position to make each stitch easily and as perfectly as anyone who is right-handed.

Take the simplified half-cross as an example. With canvas and threaded needle make the stitches with the diagram turned upside down. This way you will be starting in the upper left corner and working down the canvas.

As you pull the needle through a mesh to complete a stitch, relax your hand and follow the point of the needle. This way the yarn will drop in a natural loop. If you roll the needle slightly from the thumb over and up on your forefinger you will keep the yarn from twisting.

Never again will you have difficulty in doing any of the needlepoint stitches if you do them as directed here, and your stitches will always slant in the same direction as the design.

Using Frames for Working Needlepoint

IN EARLY TIMES almost all needlepoint was done on frames—the canvas stretched on a frame in the manner similar to the way we make hooked rugs today. The frame was usually placed across the arms of a chair or on a standard like a music rack. It was usually left by the fireplace. A chair was near so the mistress of the house could make a few stitches whenever she sat down.

Today's needlepoint is done in a much more companionable way. Canvas is flexible. It is so well meshed that you do not need to have it in a frame and you can carry it with you wherever you go.

There are a few instances, even today, where a frame is desirable. If one has an arthritic condition, making it difficult to hold the work; or in the case of a broken arm where you have only the fingers to hold with, the frame is a convenience. A few blind people do their needlepoint in a frame. Understand that with a frame it takes longer because instead of putting the needle in and bringing it out in the same pull-through, you must put it through all the way and bring it out all the way and, after all, the one time-consuming thing in making needlepoint is the pulling through of the yarn. One reason it is easy to watch television when you do needlepoint is that you only need to look while you insert the stitch.

Some use a plain 1¼″ pine picture frame and stretch their canvas over this, tacking it at the sides. Others take 4 strips of 1¼″ x ¾″ wood, sandpaper the strips, clamp them together at the corners—much like quilting frames—and use these as frames.

Some of you may have a metal "sewing bird" which you can use. Its bill catches and holds your work, giving you really a third hand. This is very convenient if one hand is incapacitated for any reason. Sometimes these little birds can be very useful because if you have a hand you cannot use for a time, but you want the therapeutic value of needlepoint, the bird can be a hand for you. This is especially appealing to children when they are doing needlepoint.

Container for Your Needlepoint

THERE ARE DOZENS of types of containers suitable for needle-point. Sewing baskets, boxes, tote bags in all their variations. The idea is to have your needlepoint always at hand so that you can make a few stitches and save yourself annoyance or irritation in waiting, so that you can relax and do the stitches when visiting, when neighbors drop in, when you wait in the car for someone to come, etc.

We have found that a little nylon bag is convenient, inconspicu-ous and easy to carry wherever you go. Make it in a color that you prefer. That is, if you wear brown or blue or black more than other colors, make your bag in that color.

Nylon Bag for Needlepoint. This neat, easy-to-make nylon bag makes a perfect container for your needlepoint.

Material required: Buy ½ yard of nylon fabric—most of it comes 45 inches wide, the least wiry quality is best. Buy 2 yards of 1-inch-wide, matching-color nylon ribbon and 1 spool of matching nylon thread.

To cut: Straighten the crosswise edges. Bring one selvage edge over 16½ inches and pin on a straight line. Cut on this line. Cut 2 strips for handles, each 18 inches long and 3 inches wide.

To make: Stitch from **A** to **B** on the bag. Pivot and then stitch from **B** to **C**, making a scant ¼-inch seam. Turn bag inside out, press the stitched line and make a French seam—a generous ¼ inch.

To make handles: Lay an 18-inch length of ribbon through the center of each handle strip. Baste, bring one edge over on the ribbon, turn in the other raw edge so it is even with the folded edge. Stitch this turned edge, then turn and stitch along opposite edge of handle.

Attach the handles: First, divide both top edges of bag in half and mark with pins as at **D**. Measure and mark 3½ inches each side of pins. From right side, pin handles to position on each side of bag, allowing ends to extend over raw edge as shown at **E**. Stitch across handles securely as at **F**.

Finish the top of bag: Lap ribbon over edge of the bag and handles as at **G** Stitch all around the bag as at **H**. Turn ribbon inside the bag and stitch along other edge of ribbon as at **I**, so stitching will show on the right side as at **J**. Press the bag.

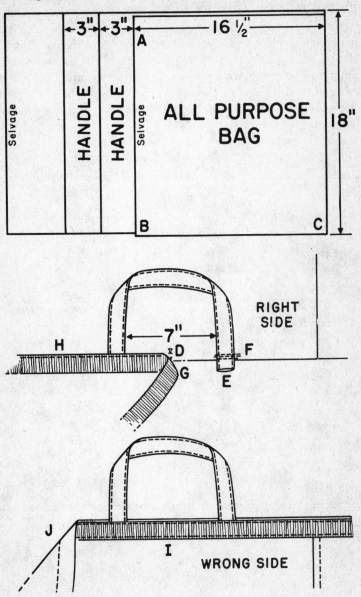

Drawings and instructions courtesy Singer Sewing Machine Co.

Decorating With Needlepoint

WHEN AN ENTIRE ROOM is decorated in needlepoint, it is well to use plain walls and plain carpeting, these to accent or harmonize in color with the background colors of the needlepoint. If both the walls and the floors are without design the needlepoint will be emphasized and appear to better advantage. Even when several pieces are covered as illustrated in the photograph below, it is advisable to have some pieces covered in plain fabric, this again for contrast.

Needlepoint Stitches

REVIEW ALL THE STITCHES given in these pages. Practice them on a small piece of canvas or on the edge of your needlepoint piece. Choose the stitch that is recommended for your purpose.

You may have learned to do some of the stitches differently because people of each nation, or even sections of a country, doing needlepoint may do the stitches with slight variations.

We have tried in these pages to find the most popular stitches, to present the easiest possible way of doing them. Study all methods and see. Perhaps you will find a quicker or easier way to do the stitches than the one used previously, and this naturally will give you more enjoyment.

If, as you work, you find any short cuts that do not take away from the beauty of your finished work or distort in any way the evenness of your stitches, do not hesitate to use these. All individuals learn to vary the techniques they use in doing handwork. If your variation simplifies the work for you or makes it more interesting, use it by all means.

Needlepoint Stitch Descriptions

OUR CHART SHOWS the favored stitches used in needlepoint. In the following pages you will find enlarged diagrams showing exactly how each of these stitches is made. Study this chart, and read the text as you follow the stitches in and out of the mesh.

There is a reason for each needlepoint stitch shown, and a reason why each is made as it is. Each stitch has a purpose and you learn to do the ones that fit your purpose best. Speed will come when you know the stitch and have enough practice. Once you are a devotee of needlepoint, you will almost be able to do it with your eyes shut.

Column 1. In the left-hand column, we show various stitches in work with the needle in place for the next stitch. The bottom square in the left column shows how tramé looks on canvas.

Column 2. Study the center column. Here you will see how the various stitches look on the right side. Look at this chart closely, note that all the stitches appear identical on the right side.

Column 3. This shows how the various needlepoint stitches appear from the back. Notice that the new half-cross (simplified) and regular half-cross have straight lines on the wrong side, which is adequate thickness for pillows, pictures and all fashion accessories. Some also like to use this stitch for chairs and couches. We recommend, however, that furniture pieces in general be made with the continental or the basket weave stitch.

The Continental Stitch. This stitch gives slightly less thickness on the front than on the back. It takes about one-quarter more yarn than does the half-cross. The extra yarn in the continental stitch provides a padding that is comparable to the pad placed under a rug.

The Basket Weave. This is worked diagonally back and forth. It makes a beautiful stitch on the wrong side, as well as on the right.

The Petit Point Stitch. The last stitch in the right-hand column is petit point. As its name implies, it is small. On the canvas it equals four stitches to one of gros point. This stitch is worked in the same way as the continental, except the regular four-ply needlepoint yarn is separated into two and the petit point is worked with these two strands.

Study the detail stitch diagrams on the following pages closely, read the instructions carefully. You will find each stitch easy to make and fascinating when applied to your canvas.

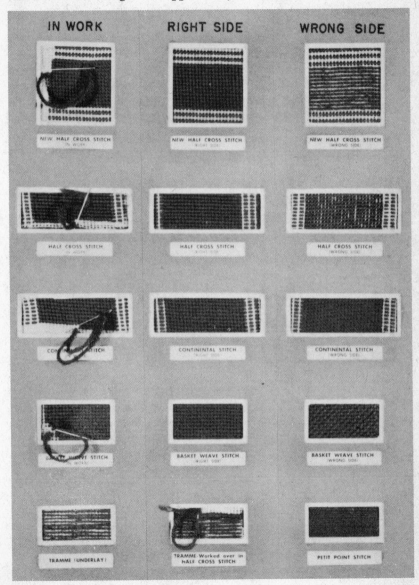

The Continental Stitch

THIS STITCH is preferred by many for furniture pieces as the yarn cushions the stitch underneath.

Work through large meshes, over double threads. Always work from right to left.

1st Row—Start on right side of canvas, upper right corner, 7 meshes outside the outlined area. Working horizontally, make 3 running stitches by inserting the needle over and under the double threads. See **A** in diagram below.

These stitches running in and out of the prescribed number of meshes are made to insure a neat beginning and ending for each row. Also, to provide a smooth flat edge for mounting. These running stitches holding securely as they do make it unnecessary

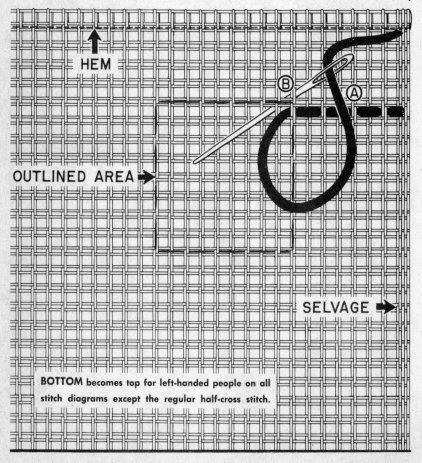

HEM

Ⓑ Ⓐ

OUTLINED AREA →

SELVAGE →

BOTTOM becomes top for left-handed people on all stitch diagrams except the regular half-cross stitch.

to hold the end of the yarn to work over it, or to make a knot.

Draw needle to right side of canvas in 1st mesh of area to be worked. Insert needle 1 mesh to right in row above and with one motion bring point of needle up in mesh directly left of first mesh where yarn is drawn to right side. See **B**. Continue across row repeating the stitch to end of outlined area, ending with needle on right side of canvas—insert needle in next large mesh to left and work over and under double threads to make 3 running stitches to end row as in **C**. Cut yarn.

2nd Row—On right-hand side of canvas, make 3 running stitches over and under corresponding double threads in large meshes directly below last row worked. Draw needle to right side of canvas in first mesh of area to be worked. Insert needle one mesh to right in row above (in same mesh as stitch in previous row). Repeat same as for Row 1. See **D**. Make 3 running stitches to end row. Cut yarn.

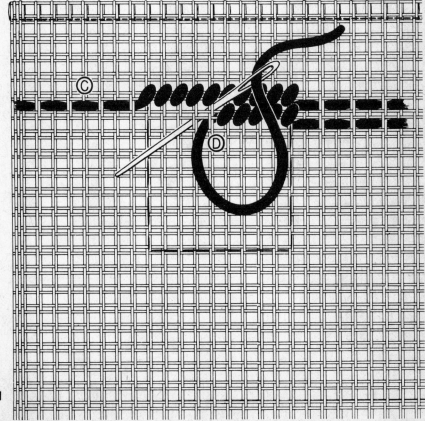

Continue working each row in the same manner, starting and ending with running stitches, filling in entire outlined area.

The illustration shows that these stitches worked inside the design, are made exactly the same as all the others; also it shows the use of short lengths of the yarn. See page 20.

The Regular Half-Cross Stitch

WORK THROUGH large meshes, over double threads. See diagram **A**. Starting in the upper left corner of canvas, 5 meshes outside outlined area, make 2 running stitches by inserting the needle over and under double threads. Draw needle to right side of

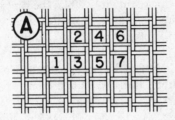

canvas at 1, insert point of needle down in 2, with one motion draw needle out in 3, continue across canvas in same manner (needle down in 4, up in 5, down in 6, up in 7, and so on). Make 2 running stitches in same manner as starting, to finish the row. Cut yarn. Make each succeeding row by returning to left side of canvas and working each row (in large meshes) exactly as first row. See diagram **B**.

If you are now using this stitch and are right handed, for more comfortable working, try turning the work around so that you work across from the right lower corner. This allows your yarn to loop below your hand and saves one motion with each stitch.

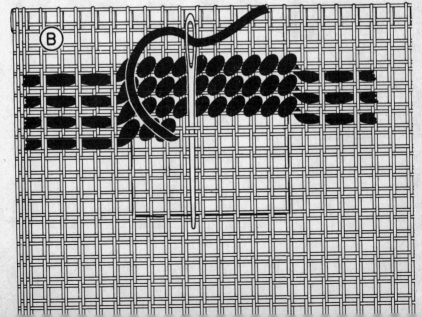

The Simplified Half-Cross Stitch

THIS STITCH has been adopted by many in place of the regular half-cross because it allows a more comfortable position for the hand, tends to let the yarn fall in a natural, untwisted loop below hand while working (retaining the original unbeaten quality of the yarn rather than wearing it). When the simplified half-cross is worked in one direction, as recommended, it is easier to block and more uniform in appearance. In addition, this stitch works up quickly.

To make the simplified half-cross stitch, work through large meshes, over double threads. Work from lower right corner straight up the canvas.

Start on the right side of the canvas, 5 meshes below the outlined area in lower right corner, make 2 running stitches by inserting the needle over and under double threads. See photograph **A**. Draw needle to right side of canvas in first mesh of area to be worked.

First Row. Insert point of needle 1 mesh to right in row above, with one motion draw needle through mesh directly left. See

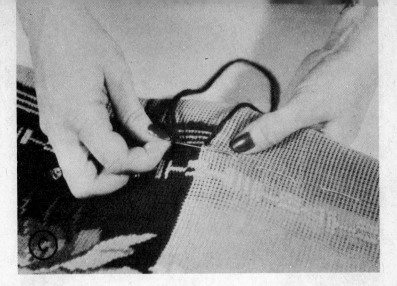

diagram **B**. Also see photographs **C**, **D**, and **E**. Notice the smooth unridged beginning that the 2 running stitches give. This method eliminates knots and gives a nice flat edge for mounting. Needle is in horizontal position—forming slanting stitch on right side and straight stitch on back of your canvas. Continue this stitch to top of outlined area. Insert needle 1 mesh to right in row above and make 2 running stitches up canvas (in same manner as starting) to finish this row. Cut yarn.

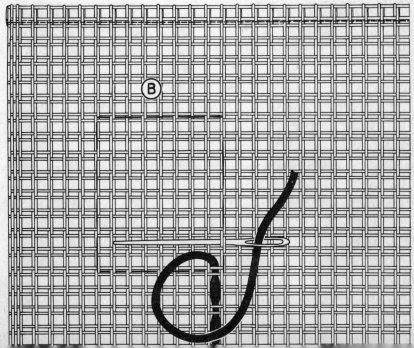

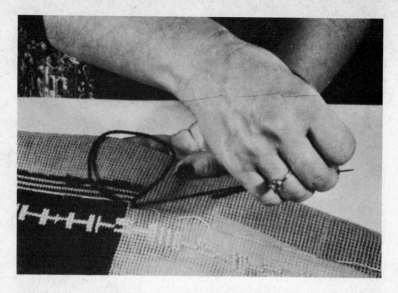

D Draw needle left in first mesh of working area, and don't fight the yarn. Allow it to fall limp to reduce twisting.

E Draw the yarn through with ONE easy graceful motion. It's relaxing for you and less wearing on the yarn.

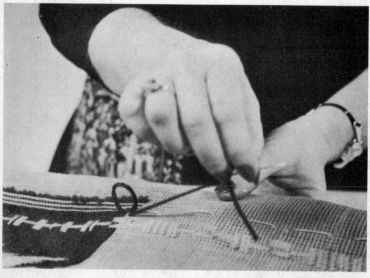

Second Row. On right side of canvas, make 2 running stitches over and under the large meshes directly left of first row. Draw needle to right side of canvas in first mesh of area to be worked. Insert needle 1 mesh to right in row above (in same mesh as stitch in previous row). Draw needle through mesh directly to left. See diagram **F**. Continue to top of outlined area and end as for row 1.

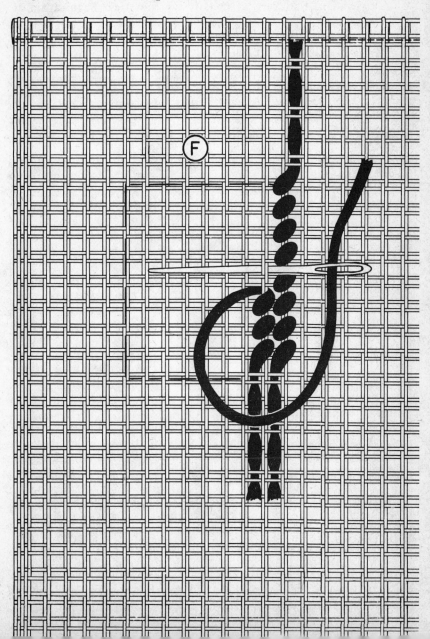

To fill the space below the design, work from the bottom up. When you reach the design, draw needle to the back and run it under threads of the design. Cut the yarn. To continue above the design, anchor your yarn under the design yarn, wrong side of course. Continue working to top of canvas as in preceding rows. Begin again at the bottom and continue this row until you reach the design. End yarn as in previous row, then begin again at upper edge of design and work toward top of canvas as before. See diagram **G**. Continue with your needlepoint until all the marked area is completed.

Ripping Out Needlepoint Stitches

IF YOU HAVE some stitches that are not good in your piece, especially the ones that you have done too quickly or those around the petit point design, rip them out carefully and replace them. It is good always to remember that a piece of needlepoint is designed and made to become an heirloom. With care it should last several lifetimes. So try to do it as perfectly as you know how and don't rush the work. Needlepoint is an art to enjoy and not to be "done with."

In ripping out imperfect or misplaced stitches no matter where, first slip a steel crochet hook under the stitches to loosen them. This, enough so that you can slip the point of a sharp-pointed scissors under and snip one stitch at a time until you have cut out all the undesirable ones. Never, never cut your canvas. Then, with your fingers or tweezers, pull the short yarn pieces out of your way. In removing stitches, rip out the half-cross from the right side, as in **A**; the continental from the wrong side.

When ripping in a row, when you approach the good stitches, do not cut these, but carefully draw them out until you get a two-inch length. To get this short length into the eye of the needle, cut a piece of paper a quarter-inch wide and one inch long. Lay the ripped cut end of yarn against the paper lengthwise. Slip the yarn and paper into the eye of the needle. See **B**. Now you are ready to put the needle through to the wrong side and to fasten off the yarn, just as though you were terminating the yarn in a row.

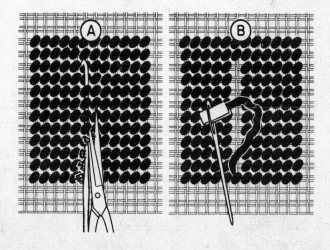

The Petit Point Stitch

PETIT POINT IS DONE the same as the continental stitch except that it is worked over every single thread, rather than over the double threads. See comparison below. For petit point stitch in work, see diagram **A**.

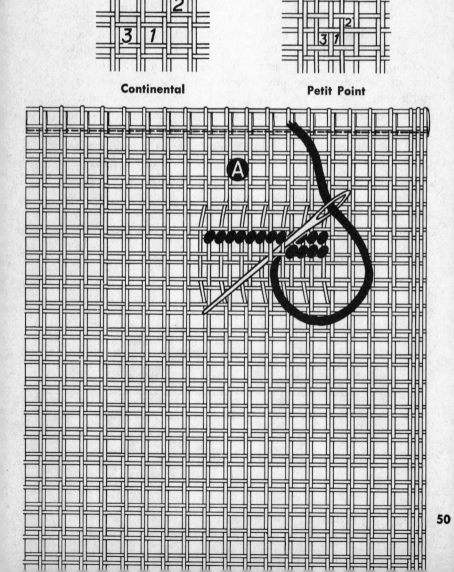

Continental

Petit Point

If center design of a piece of needlepoint is worked in the petit point stitch, it does not mean that the background should be done in petit point. In most instances, the gros point stitch is much more effective and shows off the petit point design to advantage. See photograph on page 28.

For greater ease in working close to a petit point design, insert the needle 1 mesh to right in row above, over single thread; pull needle through to the wrong side; now, bring point of needle up in mesh directly left of first mesh where yarn is drawn to right side. This takes more time than a one-motion pull-through but in small pieces around the design this is necessary as the petit point meshes are so small and close together.

With the petit point stitch you have to feel your way when close to the design. See diagram **B**.

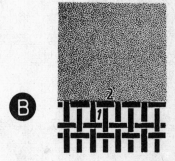

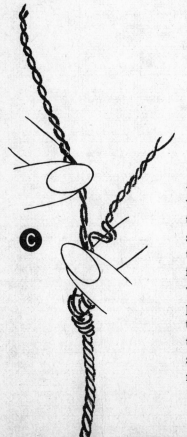

Separating Yarn. For yarn to work the petit point stitch, take two strands from your four-strand needlepoint wool. To do this, simply separate two strands from one end and hold these with the fingers of one hand and push the other two down until they are separated from the first two. See diagram **C**. These two strands go in your 22 or 24 needle.

The Basket Weave Stitch (Bias Tent)

Make a Waste Knot. Knot end of yarn. On right side of canvas, insert needle 10 meshes down from top and 10 meshes in from right edge of outlined area. (Excess yarn on back will be worked over as stitches fill the canvas. Cut knot off when stitches on right side of canvas reach the knots.)

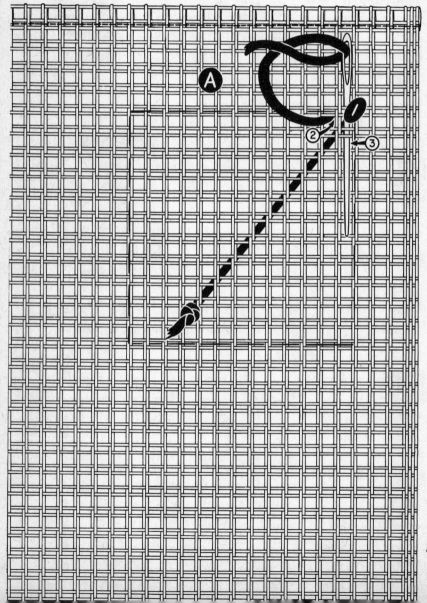

Work through large meshes, over double threads. Draw the needle to the right side of canvas in first mesh to be worked in upper right corner of outlined area. Insert needle 1 mesh to right in row above, draw needle to right side of canvas in mesh directly left of bottom of stitch 1. Holding needle vertically, insert needle 1 mesh to right in row above and draw needle through at mesh 3. See diagram **A**.

To complete third stitch—insert needle 1 mesh to right in row above, draw needle to right side in mesh 4. See diagram **B**.

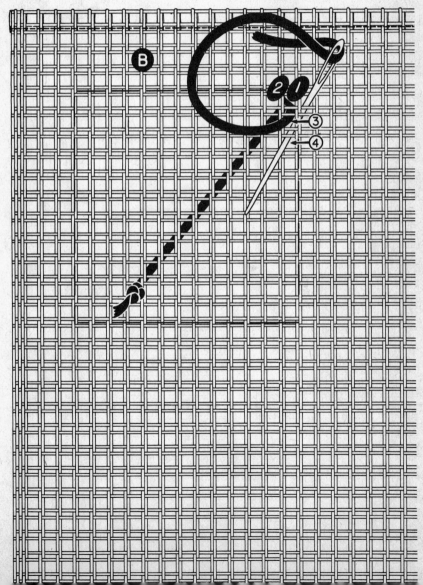

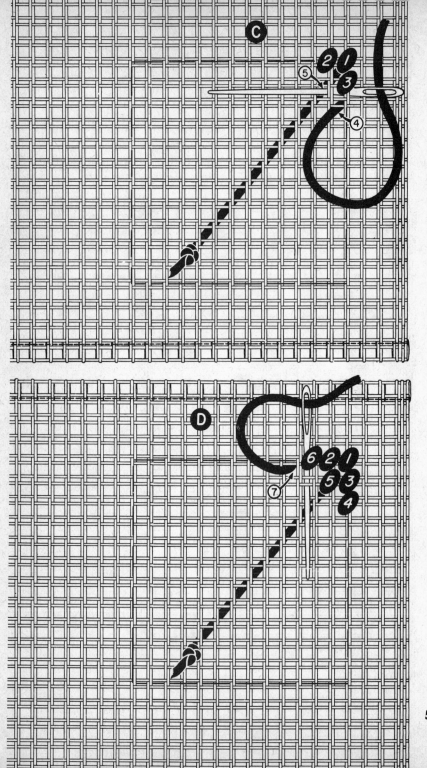

Holding needle horizontally—insert needle 1 mesh to right in row above, draw needle to right side in mesh 5. See diagram **C**.

Continue up row with needle in horizontal position. After stitch 6 completed in top row, draw needle to right side in mesh 7.

Holding needle vertically—insert needle 1 mesh to right in row above and work down canvas. See diagram **D**.

Proceed down canvas as shown on diagram **E**.

Always be sure to work 2 stitches on outside edges of outlined area, working vertically down the canvas and up horizontally.

When last stitch of first row is made, insert needle at left edge of outlined area 1 mesh to right in row above, draw needle through to back. Draw needle to right side of canvas in mesh directly below last stitch in row above. Work vertically down, inserting needle 1 mesh to right in row above, as before.

On bottom row—insert needle 1 mesh to right in row above, draw needle to right side in third mesh of this row and work up in horizontal position.

Repeat this procedure until outlined area is completed.

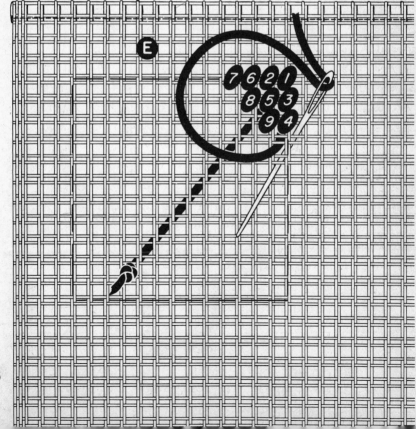

The Diagonal Stitch

THIS STITCH is fascinating to do—it is intriguing when you do a rainbow of colors across the top of a cushion or stool. It is lovely in a monotone of two or three colors—and adapts itself to geometric motifs in a most pleasing way.

To Make the Diagonal Stitch. Work through large meshes, over double threads. Begin in the lower right corner of canvas and work diagonally across canvas to top left edge of outlined area.

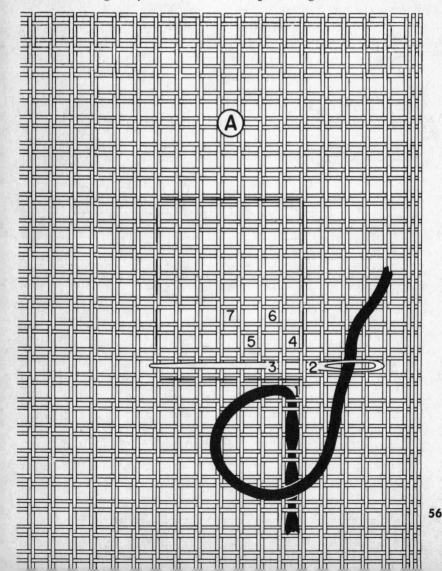

Start on the right side of the canvas, 5 meshes below the outlined area in the lower right corner, make 2 running stitches by inserting the needle over and under the double threads.

First Row. Draw the needle to the right side of the canvas in the first mesh of the area to be worked. See 1 in diagram **A**. Insert point of needle 1 mesh to right in the row above (see 2), and with one motion bring needle out at 3. Insert point of needle down in 4, up at 5. Continue diagonally across until the top row of the outlined area is reached. Finish off with 2 running stitches. See diagram **B**.

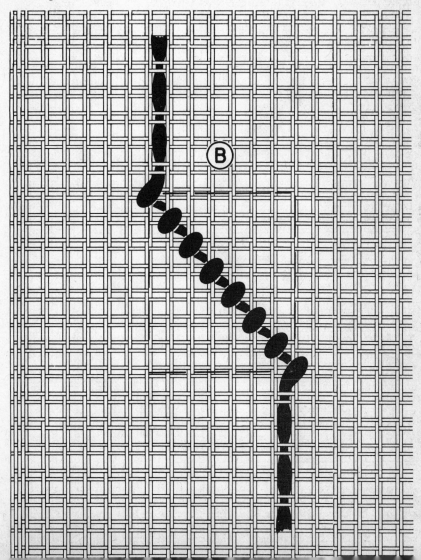

Start each row from the lower right corner in same manner as first row. Always begin each new row to the left of the previously completed row. See diagram **C**. Continue working until entire

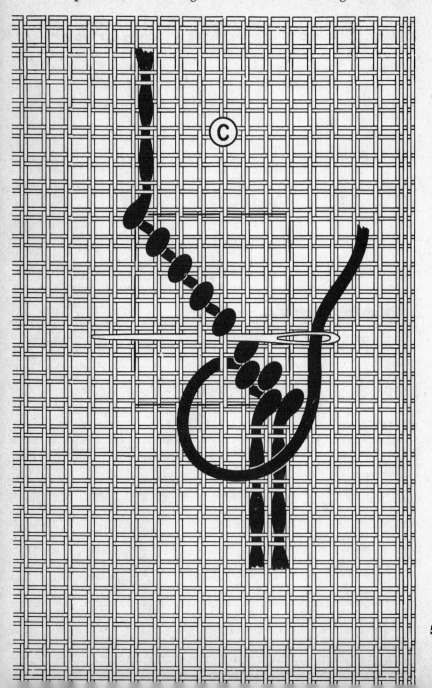

left outlined area is completely filled in. See diagram **D**. Reverse your canvas, so the top is at the bottom. Follow directions from beginning to end exactly as for first half of canvas. Turn diagram **D** upside down to see how upper half appears finished.

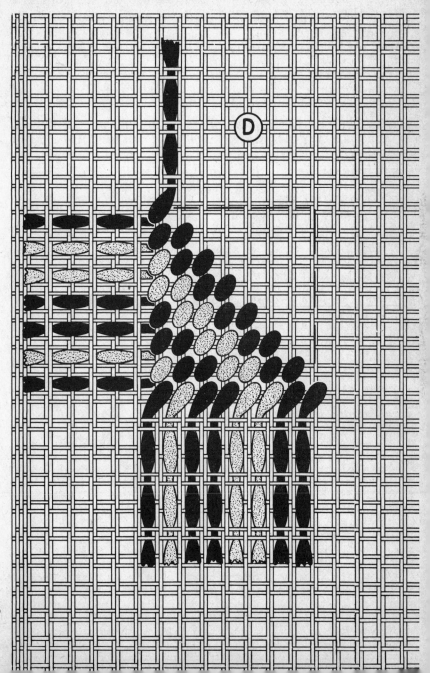

Tramé

TRAMÉ IS AN UNDERLAY of colored yarns placed over the horizontal meshes that are close together. The purpose of tramé is to indicate the design and change of colors on the canvas.

The regular half-cross stitch is worked over the tramé. As the number of stitches of a color vary in a row, turn your canvas upside down where the color ends in each row. Continue working from left to right.

All tramé pieces come complete with appropriate colors and amount of yarn required to needlepoint over the tramé underlay.

See diagram **A** which shows tramé being worked over with the regular half-cross stitch. It is worked from the upper left corner of canvas across to right with the needle placed in a vertical position for each stitch.

The Bargello Stitch

"BARGELLO" applies, in name, to a group of designs based upon needlepoint worked in counted stitches upon canvas (usually single mesh). This work was done in Italy in the seventeenth century, and is sometimes called "Florentine or flame stitches."

This stitch is worked from left to right in upright stitches over a given number of threads. See diagram **A**. This work is counted from a chart and most of the designs are arranged so that when

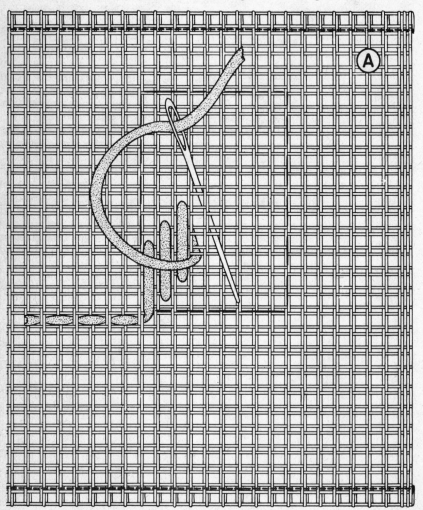

one row has been put in, practically all the counting is finished. See diagram **B**.

When the center of a row is reached, repeat the same number of stitches on the right side as you have on the left.

Bargello works on a repeat design formula and can be made in variations to suit the worker. The worker can also vary the colors of yarn to get interesting effects. For example—work one row in light blue, two in dark blue, one in gray, repeat from first row to last, varying colors as desired.

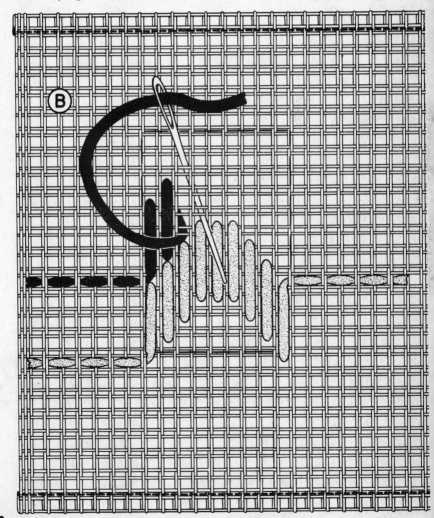

How to Block Needlepoint

AS SOON AS YOU purchase your needlepoint canvas, make a note of its measurements so when you are ready to block your piece you can draw the outside dimensions on the blocking board. (Some buy a piece of plywood three by four feet and keep it just to use for blocking.) Never cut your canvas before you block it. Use your selvages and hems as support for your tacks when blocking.

Buy long-pointed, best-quality, rustproof thumbtacks. Artist tacks are ideal. About six dozen tacks are needed for a chair or stool seat. Keep these in a box where they will be ready for your next piece. (It is our experience that before you complete a piece, you will have another on the way.) If you feel thumbtacks are too expensive, use long carpet tacks.

First, true lines are penciled on your board, with a yardstick to guide you accurately—this so that you will know what you are to stretch to. Place your needlepoint piece on a table and wet it with

water. Do not be afraid to really wet the piece. A clean wash-cloth or sponge is good for this.

Place piece wrong side out on the board. Begin at the lower right-hand corner. Stretch as you go. Stretch with firmness, but with care. Sometimes the man of the house can help with this stretching. Work at this until all four sides are true.

Place tacks a scant one inch apart. Work to the corner at the left. Make doubly sure the line is true. Then stretch the side line up to the left upper corner. Do this on the marked line and be very sure that each and every side meets the line. Now stretch to top right-hand corner. Then stretch up and place tacks all the way across the top. Finally, tack the right-hand side. This requires firm stretching to meet the line.

After the tacking is done, take a cloth and see if you can pat out any water. Your needlepoint should remain on the board until thoroughly dry.

Steaming and Pressing. When your creation is dry, remove it from the board, place a slightly damp cloth over the right side and steam ever so gently; or hold a hot steam iron about two inches above the piece and steam it thoroughly. This tends to fluff the yarn and give it a nice finish.

Blocking Professionally Done. You can take your needlepoint to art needlework shops. For a fee, they will block the piece for you. It is our experience that once you have made a beautiful piece you want to see it finished and will enjoy blocking it your-self. However, the service of experts is a great convenience when you are situated so that you cannot do this work for yourself.

Piecing Needlepoint

When to Piece Needlepoint. It is recommended that the directions on opposite page for piecing be used primarily for putting rug squares together.

When needlepoint pieces are worked and it is decided that they are to be used on a larger object than originally intended, or if for some reason the finished piece is not big enough to fit properly, it is suggested that rather than get involved in the complications of piecing the canvas, the needlepoint be combined with fabrics. See **B.** Any good upholstery fabric that will blend or contrast with the background yarn in the finished needlepoint piece, when properly attached to the canvas, will add originality and beauty to the finished object.

Don't try to piece old covers to make them fit new chairs—it will be practically impossible to obtain yarn the color of your original pieces. The elements change colors through the years and it is very rare when a new yarn can match one that has been exposed. Also it is tedious to piece (not too bad on new pieces, but very involved on used ones).

After determining placement of needlepoint piece on object to be covered, mark correct placement on upholstery fabric. Mark ¼″ or ⅜″ *inside* first outline, for seam allowance. Cut out center

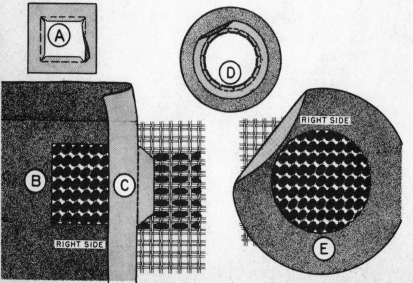

and clip corners **A.** If fabric is not very firm, make tailored corners. Turn fabric edges under **B** and pin over needlepoint. Slip-baste turned edge to needlepoint. Back-stitch along seamline from wrong side of fabric **C.**

If a round or oval edge is used over needlepoint, cut paper pattern in desired shape and mark upholstery fabric accordingly. Cut ⅜" *inside* marked outline. Finish with fitted facing, **D** turn facing to wrong side and press. Lay over needlepoint and slip-stitch to place **E.**

How to Piece Needlepoint

THE PIECE OF CANVAS to be added must be exactly the same mesh size as that of the piece of needlepoint. Cut off the selvages, or open the hems in both canvases.

The double threads that are closest together in a piece of canvas should always run vertically. Be sure that they match when piecing. The illustrations shown are of a horizontal piecing.

Overcast the seam edges of your two pieces separately. Place the right sides of these two overcast pieces of canvas together to make a seam. Do this so the canvas meshes match and appear as one. Pin, then baste these canvases together in preparation for a five-eights-inch deep seam. Use a strong linen thread, or a thread drawn from the canvas. Backstitch over the double vertical threads, as at **A.**

For best results and to be sure you are between the double horizontal threads on both pieces of canvas, use two distinct movements of the needle in making your backstitches—one down through canvas—then one up through canvas. A single thread of each piece will be drawn together, and appear as at **B.** Press

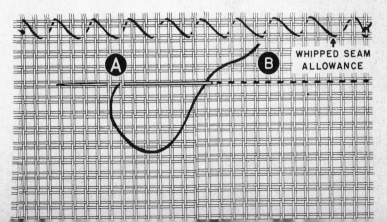

WHIPPED SEAM ALLOWANCE

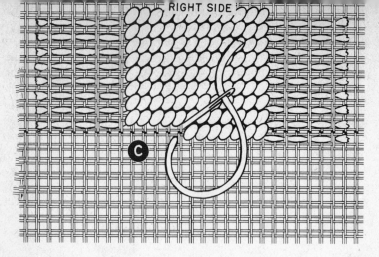

seam open. Consider the right side of this seamline as one row
of mesh when needlepointing over it.

Start working from where you left off on your original needlepoint piece on the right side, and proceed down the canvas until
the backstitched row is reached. While working these rows, take
care that you do not work in the seam allowances on the wrong
side. Hold these away as you work so that you cannot catch them.

When the pieced row is reached, again use two distinct movements of the needle when making your stitch—one down through
the canvas, all the way through one of the seam allowances—
then draw the needle to the right side of the canvas up through
the other seam allowance and continue your stitches to complete
the row.

Diagram **C**. This diagram shows how stitches should be worked
after the two canvases have been seamed together (using the
continental stitch as an example).

Diagram **D**. This is the back of the pieced canvas and shows
the only row where continental stitches have been worked
through the seam allowances' double thicknesses.

When working rows immediately below joined row do not work
through seam allowances.

See photograph **E** and notice that the needlepoint stitches that
are worked over the seam on the left-hand side have a tendency
to be lower than the adjoining rows. To raise these stitches so they
are uniform and in line with the others, we recommend you use
the needlepoint yarn double. When the continental stitch is used,
start at the right edge of the pieced row and draw the needle

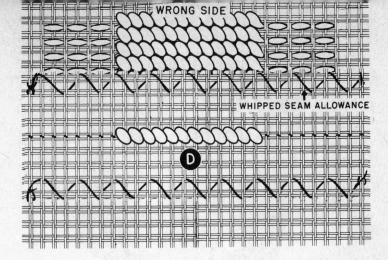

WRONG SIDE

WHIPPED SEAM ALLOWANCE

D

under the worked stitches. (Draw your needle under about 7 stitches at a time.) Continue in this way across the row, making sure the double yarn is under every stitch. Cut the yarn flush with first and last stitches. In photograph **E**, if you examine closely, you will see that the yarn has been drawn under the stitches on the right side and not under those on the left. Note evenness of stitches in seamed row on the right-hand side with rows above and below. The left-hand side, as you see, is slightly lower. When the double yarn shown is drawn under these stitches the entire row will be uniform.

When adding a piece of canvas to the side or vertically, the piecing is done in the same manner (working in between the double vertical threads).

E

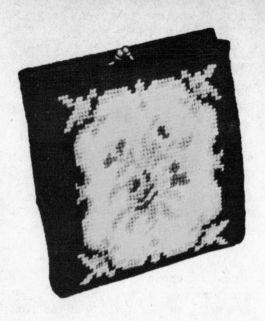

How to Use and Mount Needlepoint

YOU WILL FIND as you get acquainted with the versatility of needlepoint that it fits in and is right for many purposes.

You will see needlepoint used, appropriately, on a chaise longue and on boudoir chairs. On library, living room and dining room chairs in classic or modern design, with light or dark backgrounds, all designed to fit in with any décor.

Use needlepoint on screens (both decorative and for the fireplace) and on cornices for draperies. Brooches to wear are enjoyed by many, as are tote, evening and daytime bags. Pockets for dresses, also collars and cuffs, are frequently in the fashion picture.

Rugs, pillows, bellpulls, doorstops, decorative and motto pictures, hangings and cushions—there are scores of uses for needlepoint. Your responsibility is to choose the design that is appropriate to your need—the colors right for your use—then part of you will go into making articles that will do you proud.

Needlepoint for Framing

WHEN MOUNTING a piece of needlepoint for framing, block the piece according to blocking instructions on page 64.

A needlepoint picture must be blocked true, especially the needlepoint rows at the edges of the picture, so that the finished piece will fit evenly into a frame and appear true on all edges.

We assume you have a suitable frame. If you must buy a frame, measure your piece carefully and get one that will fit, or take your piece to a framer and have him frame your picture for you.

For a successful framing job at home cut a piece of cardboard a scant one-eighth inch smaller on all four sides than the glass in the frame. This is to allow needlepoint to be turned over the edges of the cardboard and then to be fitted back of the glass.

A square wallet. such as shown at top of opposite page, has many uses. The package comes complete with lining, frame, all. Keep the printed instructions that you receive with any packaged item of needlepoint, so that when your canvases are complete you will know exactly how to assemble the finished article. This is particularly necessary for bags, eyeglass cases, belts and such.

Pillows

NEEDLEPOINT PILLOWS are favored by many for couches, chairs or chaise longues, even for the top of a footstool that needs more height.

If you have chairs with hard wooden seats, make flat cushions for these. Tie the cushions to the backs of the chairs with silken cord finished with tassels. They may be lined with thin foam rubber to make them comfortable and practical.

Buy a ready-made pillow and make a needlepoint top to fit it. Turn the four edges of the needlepoint, trim away any surplus. Press neatly, especially at the corners. Catch the top to the pillow, using small whipping stitches and matching thread. Be sure to pin the top to place first, then baste all edges carefully so that the top cannot slip out of position during the whipping.

You may make a pillow to a size to fit your needlepoint. (Many have down cushions they would like to reshape and re-cover.) For this, use ticking for the inside that holds the down, and a suitable fabric for one side and for the box edges of the cushion. Cover a cord with a true bias of your fabric. Make your pillow cover, press carefully. Slip the pillow to place. Square out all corners nicely, then slip-stitch the opening together.

Fringe is often used on needlepoint pillows. To make a fringe, see page 94. Use the same yarn as you use for the background stitches, or one to match a color in the design. Insert the fringe in the seam exactly as you would a cord.

If you use foam rubber for the filling of your pillows, make sure that the rubber is ½″ larger on all four sides than the exact cushion size—this so that it will hold true to the edges. The foam rubber can be held in slightly, and you do want a true, unwrinkled box edge with this type of filling. The square pillow shown above is kapok filled and is not as firm as a foam rubber cushion should be on the edges.

Applying Needlepoint to Slip-Seat Chairs

WHEN YOUR NEEDLEPOINT has been blocked, examine the seat of the chair. Be sure that it is firm and without sag. If the chair has a plywood bottom, examine the top padding; in fact, build it up slightly in the center, evenly of course. (If the chair is new and of good workmanship, this is not necessary.)

If the chair has a burlap upholsterer's tape crisscrossed on the bottom, check to make sure this is very tight. Take out the tacks if necessary and stretch until tapes are tight. In an old chair replace the old tapes with new ones, because you are placing the needlepoint to be used for a long time and a good foundation for it is essential.

When your needlepoint piece is blocked, ready for mounting, lay any left-over yarn from your last skein under the needlepoint piece. This is a precaution, so if your piece is cut, stained or burned, the right yarn will be readily available to make repairs. This yarn will match more nearly than anything you can buy.

Place the design of your needlepoint so that the top of the design goes toward the back. Center the design exactly on the top of the seat. Pin it at the four corners so that it cannot slip. Then, turn the seat over, bring the two sides over, and place a tack at each corner through the canvas and into the wood. Add

tacks along the way every two or three inches until the sides are held securely. Now bring the front end up and tack it to position. Turn the corners in so that you get a very neat turn exactly at the corner. See photograph **A**. Tack the front edge to place. Lastly, bring the back of the seat cover up over the edge and tack it.

If there is a notch at each corner of the back, simply fit the

needlepoint into this notch. See photograph **B**. You will see how nicely it comes in without cutting. Tack it down tightly around the notch on the underside. After the seat is very tight and tacked on all four sides, place more tacks about one and a half inches part. Now place the lining over the entire bottom, using tacks from four to six inches apart.

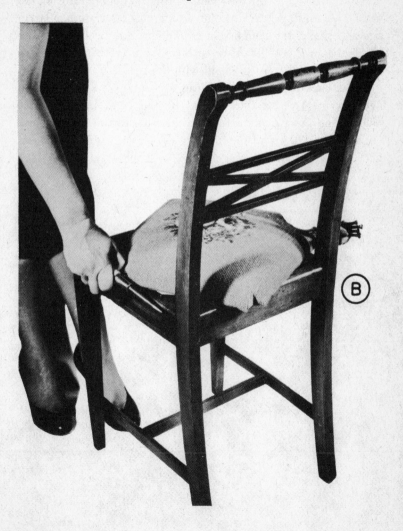

Chairs with Needlepoint Seat and Back

FREQUENTLY WE SEE side chairs with seats and backs in harmonizing needlepoint design, as shown. These are available in pairs.

Notice that although the chairs in the photograph are of the same type, and the needlepoint designs on each are similar in size and shape, the bouquets are different. The background can be identical for both chairs or each can be made with a different color background yarn to blend with the other.

If the back of the chair requires a covering, do this in plain needlepoint. You can buy canvas by the yard. Use the same background color as used for the chair itself. You can also use upholsterer's velvet for the back in a color to match or contrast with the needlepoint on the chair.

Nail or Gimp Finish

WHEN THE SEAT is a permanent part of the object, then it is necessary to use upholstery nails to fasten the needlepoint to place. Upholstery nails come by the box, shiny brass or oxidized finish. They also come in colors. Choose the kind best suited to your needlepoint.

Buy upholsterer's gimp in a color as near your background yarn as possible. The gimp should be exactly as wide as your tacks.

First, stretch the needlepoint securely. Place a row of sharp pointed tacks one-half inch above the finish or fitted line of the needlepoint.

Trim the needlepoint to the exact edge. Use a razor blade or very sharp scissors for this. Cut with great care. When the edge is true, place the gimp, which is exactly the width of the brass tacks, over the cut edge. Apply the gimp with fabric glue; then place the ornamental tacks as close together as possible all around the four sides of the chair.

If gimp is used without the tacks, place the fabric glue on the back of the gimp, a few inches at a time, keeping it back from the edges. Place and gently stretch the gimp to place.

Tack the gimp, applying glue as you tack, so that it will not smear woodwork of the chair or your needlepoint. Use tacks with invisible heads for this final tacking. To finish, lap the gimp at a back corner.

Chaise Longue

A CHAISE LONGUE may be covered in one long piece as shown, or in two sections, or needlepoint may be used on the back only and fabric used for the rest. A scatter or all-over design is good for a piece of furniture as large as a chaise longue.

Notice how the cushion in this case has a corded edge—regular upholsterer's cording or gimp is used for finishing. It is best to match the background color of the needlepoint when using cording, fringe or braid to finish.

In a fitted piece such as at the foot, as in the one shown, your needlepoint needs to be cut very precisely to fit. If you have an automatic zigzagger sewing machine or attachment, go over the edges with this to prevent fraying of yarn ends. Lacking such, a row or two of plain machine stitching done with a short stitch is helpful. Until you are expert in applying fitted upholstery, you will be safest if you have a professional do it for you.

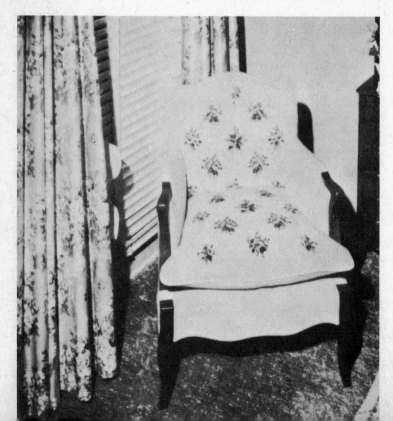

Fire Screens

NEEDLEPOINT HAS BEEN used for fire screens for centuries. Shown here is an especially good example.

Choose a frame right for your room—then buy a piece of needlepoint with a design appropriate to other furnishings in your room. Give special consideration to the background yarn color. The color should be right for the fireplace itself, your room and its furnishings. Avoid drab colors.

The needlepoint should be applied to the screen the same as to a chair, using gimp and brass-headed tacks placed as shown.

Benches

Here are two examples of all-over or scatter designs—a slip-seat for the spinet, a hobnail cover for the dressing table stool. Notice

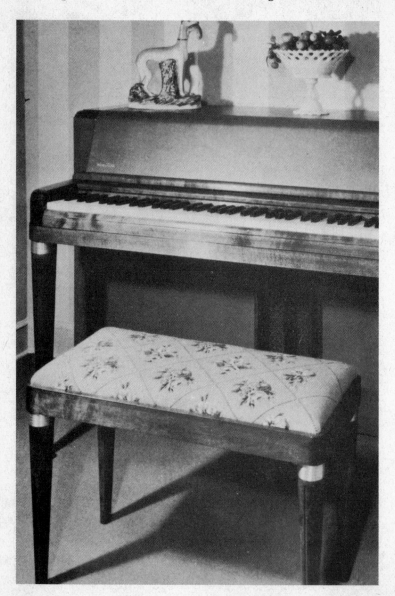

how perfectly these are done; also the neatness of the turns at corners and edges.

Choose a design that pleases you, a background color right for your room, and make your needlepoint to serve perfectly for any room in your house. See additional designs on next two pages.

A stool such as shown here has a slip seat. You simply measure the seat, make your needlepoint to fit and then apply it to the seat as you would on a slip-seat chair.

85

Doorstops

NEEDLEPOINT DOORSTOPS usually come packaged: canvas, yarn, frame—all ready for working. Some like to buy canvas and work the family initial in and cover a brick with this to make a stop. Others make needlepoint pieces to re-cover doorstops that they already have. Needlepoint doorstops make ideal gifts.

Luggage Racks

PERHAPS YOU HAVE a luggage rack you can antique or enamel like the one shown, or you can buy one at your local furniture department. Simply make the three strips of needlepoint. Bring the edges together on the underside, cover with a strip of fabric. Tack the needlepoint right over any straps that are already there. Usually ready-made straps are narrow and easily covered.

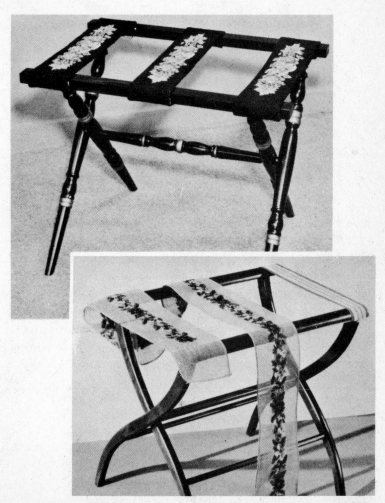

Fashion Accessories
Bags, Purses, Billfolds, Eyeglass Cases
Pockets, Belts and Scuffs

OFTEN MANUFACTURERS package the above items complete. The needlepoint piece to be worked, yarn, lining, and frames or form of fastening are usually provided in the package with the canvas. When the package is complete, there are instructions for assembling, as in examples 1, 2 and eyeglass case 3.

If you buy a piece without a frame, take your finished needlepoint, with a suitable lining, to a bag maker and have him put your handwork together with a frame, as in 4 and 5. This is usually done at a nominal price, in a professional way. You can usually find the name of such a firm in the yellow pages of your telephone book.

To make a belt, use the half-cross stitch so it won't be too thick. Be sure to make the belt long enough for your waistline. Belt kits are available with buckles, lining yarn, everything you need for making.

If you have a nice buckle, you can make the belt of a width to go with it. Lacking a buckle, you can sew grosgrain ribbon to each end of the belt. Make a tailored bow and use hooks and eyes underneath for fastening.

Pockets and collars of needlepoint or petit point are liked by many women. After you choose the design that appeals to you, use a background color suitable to the fabric on which you will use such work.

Linings in such items should be easy so as not to tighten the outside, but should always be back far enough from the edges so that it will not show outside. A semi-sheer, limp fabric makes the best lining.

Scuffs may be made of bellpull or belt strips worked to size, strips lined and attached to ready-made soles. Most art needle-work departments have soles ready for straps to be applied. In some instances they have the scuff, straps, yarn—all assembled in a package with the soles ready for making.

Needlepoint lasts for years, so choose a good quality lining and frames, so that your product will be lovely always. Remember needlepoint can be cleaned with any good cleaning fluid.

Needlepoint Pockets

Buy a design that appeals to you. Some of the small Vertès pieces make lovely pockets. The one shown was designed for a bag and made on fine white canvas. The remaining half of the bag was worked in a different colored floss to become a pocket on another dress. The bag gusset can be used as a cuff on gloves or as a mandarin collar.

The outline stitches for the bag were removed to make the pocket larger. The background was filled in with the simplified half-cross worked in floss and the piece was blocked. Edges were trimmed, and the pocket was lined throughout. It was then slip-stitched at a becoming position on the dress. If the top is cupped a little when pinned to place, it will give emphasis to the pocket, which is desirable.

Needlepoint Rugs

RUGS MADE from torn strips are called "rag rugs." Those made from strips of wool, blankets, and old apparel and braided are called "braided rugs." There are also "hooked rugs," with the yarn or narrow strips of fabric hooked through burlap. Then there are "needlepoint rugs" done the same as a needlepoint chair or cushions, the difference being in the size of the yarn and in the size of the mesh of the canvas.

When deciding on a design for a needlepoint rug, consider its suitability to your other furnishings, and choose the background color with the idea of a "show piece" that will add only beauty to your room.

A needlepoint rug, like all good needlepoint, is an investment, one to last for a lifetime. The salesgirl will help you decide the amount of yarn that you will need for the size of rug you wish to make.

To Make Fringe for a Rug

USE YOUR RUG YARN for this. Fringe can be made in two ways. **1.** The easiest is to decide the width you want, adjust your Singer craft guide to this width. Follow the written instructions that come with the guide for making it. **2.** Cut cardboard strips the width you want the fringe, plus one-half inch for seams. Wind your rug yarn around this strip, laying each row of yarn neatly flat on the cardboard. Wind and make as much fringe as you need to go around your rug or just across the ends. Use a long stitch and heavy-duty thread on your machine, or back stitch by hand, stitching one-quarter inch from one edge. Cut and carefully pull the cardboard away after stitching.

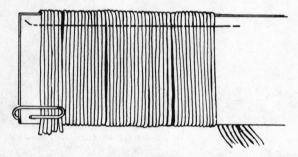

If you do use fringe all the way around, ease it at the corners so there is enough fringe to make flat corners.

The fringe usually is cut, but some prefer the uncut loop.

Needlepoint on Your Vacation

IF YOU ARE GOING AWAY to sit in the sun, to rest at the beach, or to sit while your husband plays golf, skis or attends meetings, by all means take along a lovely piece of needlepoint. Something that will do you proud when people see and remark about it. Say, "Yes, I'm doing this for a hall chair (or for my bedroom or for a cushion for the couch)." Show others how easy needlepointing is and how pleasant. There is really no needle-work that you need less equipment for, and with this you can talk and work. We don't advise needlepoint for bridge, because we insist that the dummy should watch every play, but for visiting, traveling, waiting and vacationing, needlepoint is ideal.

Try it and see!

Religious Pictures

THERE ARE TREASURED RELIGIOUS PICTURES available on needlepoint canvases. Some women enjoy making their own designs entirely, using Bible pictures that they especially like. See how to do this on page 118.

The Last Supper, which we show, is an example of the beauty of religious designs. When beautifully done in needlepoint this is a work of art on a par with an Old Master's painting. If interested in obtaining such, inquire about it at your art needlework department. If they do not have this canvas, they can possibly order it for you.

Because of the many colors used, this piece comes to you in tramé form, with the heads done in appliqué petit point. The tramé stitches, indicating the appropriate colors to be used, make it easier for you to finish your picture.

Appliqué Petit Point. This is a very fine canvas applied right over the regular canvas. Then it is worked with the tiniest possible stitches (over fifteen hundred stitches to the square inch). These stitches are worked through both canvasses. Because the stitches are so fine, details that only a paintbrush could ordinarily accomplish are thus possible.

This appliqué petit point technique is used by highly skilled specialists in this work. Their stitches are made to achieve facial expressions comparable to painting. An example of this type needlepoint was used on the heads in the Last Supper shown here. This technique is used on most fine detailed pieces that are needlepoint interpretations of famous paintings.

You Can Teach Needlepoint

MANY SCHOOLS open their classrooms for adult education. You can, with this book, become a needlepoint expert and teach the subject.

See if you cannot, with the aid of the school principal, organize a needlepoint class for one evening each week. You can handle from twelve to twenty students with the easy-to-use stitch instructions provided in this book.

Read aloud from the book to answer questions to your class. The index will help you to find quickly the answer to any question.

Friendships are developed in working with small groups of people. You will feel you are helping someone else and can enjoy it all yourself.

When teaching, do stay human. Be dignified, yes, but always kindly. Don't be aloof, be one with your class. When teaching needlepoint, as with any other subject, remember you too were taught by someone and the things you now do so easily may once have been strange to you.

Never allow the person you are teaching to feel inferior to you mentally—particularly if he does not grasp quickly what you are saying. Too often knowledge of our subject causes us to assume that the simple steps should be quickly learned by our students. A pleasant way to start a course is by telling your students that the things you are going to show them, while they seem easy for you, weren't too easy as you learned them. Ask all students of your class to assume they have never done needlepoint before, even if they have; and so all will learn basic fundamentals and they will realize that even fundamentals can be easy if taught properly.

Some students will require patience on your part. Some learn more slowly, so be simple, explicit, helpful and encouraging. You will be delighted with the reward in genuine satisfaction that such teaching will bring to you.

Be alert for magazine and newspaper articles about items on needlepoint. Watch for notices of exhibitions at museums and department stores. Once you establish your interest in this subject, you will be aware of the many opportunities you will have to learn more about it.

There is some brief history about needlepoint in this book. Read it, be able to tell your students about it, use it in conversation with your friends. Seek further information at your local library or museum. Everything you learn will arouse interest and prove helpful to you.

In this book we show in photographs a number of examples of work done by students of the Baldwin, Long Island, High School evening class. Anyone doubting his own ability to needlepoint should see this class in action. Their work is truly beautiful and their enthusiasm is high for all phases of the art.

Teaching Needlepoint to Club Groups. Needlepoint is a form of stitchery that appeals to all types of girls, especially to those who appreciate neatness, order and beauty as do our Girl Scouts.

Needlepoint and TV

SOME SAY "FIDDLESTICKS!" when told they can watch TV and needlepoint at the same time. They are sure they would miss the murder—or why someone slammed the door and left in a huff—or screeched in horror! Not so at all—you can place your needle in the flick of an eye, bring it through your needlepoint canvas in one motion. Many, many do beautiful needlepoint work and never miss a turn in the TV story. Try it yourself and you will find it completely easy.

And as for music, needlepoint allows you to keep in "tune" with it, and to enjoy both even more than when having either alone.

You need a little light for TV—and a little for needlepoint. They synchronize perfectly.

Children Enjoy Doing Needlepoint

ENCOURAGE YOUR CHILDREN to do needlepoint, at the story hour whether at home or at the library—when visitors are in or when the family are together for TV. Needlepoint is wonderful work for a rainy day—especially if you have some appealing music or a good story ready to read to them.

Start a piece in time to make a gift for a grandparent, or favorite aunt or uncle for a birthday or Christmas gift. Make sure each child knows *how*. Show, explain and start them right.

The simplified half-cross stitch is so easy for children to do. Start them with this first.

Choosing a Right Design. Buy a piece that is small enough to get done in a fairly short time. If possible let your child choose the design and background color, then it will really seem like his piece. If you have one child, buy a piece for a playmate. It is fun for two or more to do such work together.

Easy Steps. Start the piece on the marked edge, let each child practice for a few rows until he has the rhythm of the stitch and just the right tautness in each stitch. Perhaps for a first piece you should fill in around the design, but teach the child how as you do this, so he may learn to do this himself for the next piece.

Instructions and Encouragement. Watch carefully, look at the work frequently until the child gets the idea. Help at the start, have him finish a row as you watch. Show how to begin with a new needleful in the middle of a row. But, when helping, by all means have the child see how you do these things so that after the first few rows, your instructions will be understood and the child completely on his own. Too much help, as with too much criticism, is to be avoided. After all, you want the child to have the satisfaction of doing the piece on his own.

Vertès

ONE OF THE MOST IMPORTANT THINGS that has happened to needlepoint since its inception is the contribution made by Marcel Vertès. Vertès could fill a *Who's Who* all his own, having won two Oscars for his sets and costume designs. He has illustrated some thirty books. His murals are in the main lobby of the Museum of Modern Art in Paris and adorn the walls of the Peacock Lounge of the Waldorf-Astoria Hotel in New York. His work is in a half-dozen museums. He is an artist of international renown.

Vertès, a Hungarian, made his home in Paris. When he had to leave because of the German invasion, his little European car would hold only his wife, his dog and a suitcase. He wanted something from his home and he picked up the seat from his favorite chair and brought it to America with him. This chair was covered with a piece of needlepoint bought in the Flea Market of Paris. He bought it originally because it reminded him

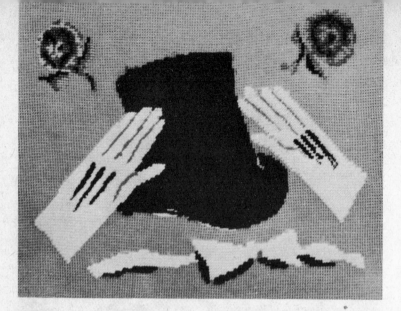

of his boyhood home in Budapest. Carmel Snow, the famous fashion editor of *Harper's Bazaar*, and herself an enthusiastic needlepointer, saw this piece in his studio and urged him to try his hand at some refreshing designs. Despite all his sadness, his designs are gay and lighthearted, some displaying real mischief. All are beautiful. The lovely three-panel screen we show below has been bought by many people who want only the finest in their homes. He has made designs for chairs, benches, footstools, cushions, and has created a number of beautiful pictures—all just for fun.

His wife Dora has herself worked many of his designs. They own a number and treasure them almost beyond anything else that they have. Vertès designs are international in their appeal. The quality is synonymous with his great ability as an artist.

Lovers of needlepoint will treasure Vertès' needle-painting and will be enchanted with his completely sophisticated approach to this previously traditional medium. His creations are the realization of the wishful thinking of young and old alike. Ask to see a Vertès piece the next time you shop for needlepoint. You will be entranced with it.

Many Men Are Needlepoint Experts

IN WORKING IN OCCUPATIONAL THERAPY, it has been our experience that men have a hesitancy to take up work which they feel belongs to a woman. Once this is overcome and a man becomes proud of his work, he will enjoy needlepoint more than any of the needlecrafts because it is easy and delightful to do, and is decidedly rewarding.

In hospitals you have to persuade men to brag about their needlework to doctors and nurses. Rather they are inclined to slip it under the cover when these notables are near. If two or three men are working at the same time, then there can be comparison of progress and a rivalry stimulated that is good for all.

Every ulcer victim should take up needlepoint. One man says,

"I pray with each stitch. It helps me—I put in many a prayer with each row of needlepoint." One man whose eyes do not allow reading does needlepoint while his wife reads to him.

Needlepoint isn't "sissy." It is relaxing, interesting and worth while. Try it out, you men. Buy a piece and begin it. Do it secretly, if you must, at first. We guarantee it will be only the beginning. Soon you will be bragging and showing your hand-work with a pride and satisfaction that is sure to influence the most stubborn.

We give here a few examples—to inspire you menfolk.

The hobby of Dr. Peter Goldstoff is needlepoint. He has made many beautiful pieces. The chair opposite, for example. The

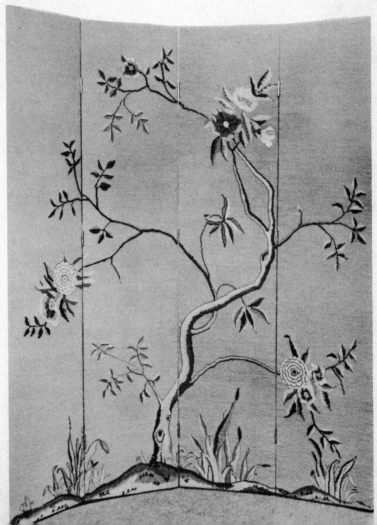

tenseness of his profession makes him appreciative of needle-point.

Robert Ellis, retired engineer, has designed unusual pieces of needlepoint. Screens, one shown below and one on previous page (typical of the Orient), rugs in Early American. He makes an engineering project of a piece, carries it through with precision, and invariably ends up with a masterpiece.

A Conversation Making Vest. The gentleman who designed and made this beautiful needlepoint vest is a stickler for detail. Notice first the shape, then the stripes, then the buttons; then—from left to right—cigar and glasses, pen, pencils and ruler. Lower pockets: black book or bill fold, theater tickets and money, plus a watch

chain with an initial charm. Note the maker's name with the year of making. A truly lovely example of an individualized piece showing ingenuity, originality and good design.

Anyone wishing to depict their personal preferences could design a vest and, by taking great pains, make it unusual and interesting as is this one.

To complete a needlepoint vest for wearing. Either cut a pattern from a vest the owner has, or pin a piece of paper over his back and cut a pattern. Cut the back from sateen, lining back and front in the same fabric. Allow 1¼ inch seams at underarm in case vest needs to be let out. Because there is no center front opening, have the vest open down the center back, hooked at the neck line and buckled or tied at waistline.

Or slant the underarm down to the waistline, use ¼ inch elastic at neck to hold the front points, and a ¾ inch elastic at the natural waistline across the back only, then the vest can be slipped on and off over the head.

Needlepoint in Occupational Therapy

MEN IN VETERANS' HOSPITALS especially like to do work with their hands; many become expert. They are easy to teach, learn quickly, and are appreciative of any new kind of work brought to them.

Most convalescents enjoy doing handwork. If you visit a hospital, or a person recovering at home, take along a piece of needlepoint and teach the stitches. The diagonal stitch is a favorite with men because they can do tailored pieces, which seem to them a little more masculine than the floral center ones.

When helping in hospitals, if the patient has to lie flat, choose a small piece of needlepoint: an eyeglass case, a pocket for a dress, a belt, collar or a small picture. Choose something that will not be heavy, to tire too much.

If the patient can sit up, then any piece will do that is not cumbersome: chair and bench seats, cushions, anything he wants to make.

A bag made of plastic or nylon that the work will fit into easily is good. It can be laid aside and reached quickly.

Plan the needlepoint for use. Encourage the worker to make it as a gift, perhaps a surprise gift. Be sure to provide everything needed—enough yarn for the background, scissors, a cork for the points and a thimble. A thimble speeds the work, protects the finger, and is indeed professional. These reasons should help to sell the idea of using a thimble. Try it!

Show the patient how to slip the needle through the mesh so it will not become lost when putting the work aside. It is a good idea to start a new needleful and lock it in place, before handing it over to the patient. Then the needle will be held securely.

Loan this book to a patient, have him read about needlepoint, what it is, its enduring beauty and long life, the variety of stitches that can be made, etc., to encourage interest and create a desire to make beautiful pieces. Avoid anything drab or dreary. Make sure the piece, the background yarn and the purpose all have appeal.

When Needlepoint Can Help You

IF YOU ARE WEARY, worried, apprehensive, buy a piece of needlepoint. It will calm you, interest you, rest you and quiet your fears. Try it and see.

By all means, choose a pretty piece and a lovely background color. Make it for someone who will enjoy using it to re-cover a chair, or as a pillow for a couch or an easy chair. Make it for a gift you will be proud to give.

Look at all the beautiful pieces, classic or modern, and find a piece that you will enjoy making.

Needlepoint is now being used with wrought iron. It is also ideal for a piano or sewing machine or dressing table bench; perfect for chairs, especially the modern types. Look, select a satisfying piece, make it and enjoy the whole of it.

Take your needlepoint with you in the car—when tired of scenery, work a row or two. Take it on train or bus, take it when visiting the neighbors or relatives. Take it with you when on vacation.

Let your needlepoint serve you as a companion: one that can comfort but not talk back.

Many Notables Do Needlepoint

MARY MARTIN, waiting for a cue in the wings of the long-run play *South Pacific*, invariably had a piece of needlepoint in her hands. She made pieces as gifts for her friends and especially for her mother-in-law, whom she adores and who appreciates Mary's efforts.

Katherine Cornell, star of *The Dark Is Light Enough*, chooses to do needlepoint as she thinks over her problems of the play. The greatly loved Helen Hayes and Peggy Wood of *I Remember Mama* fame are great enthusiasts. These popular stars almost always have pieces on hand to work on. Helen Hayes says she feels sorry when a piece is finished because she has become so fond of it in the course of finishing.

Betty Furness has done some magnificent pieces for her own home, says she loves doing each piece, and proves it by having several in work at a time. She often makes her own designs simply because of the fun of doing them. Jane Froman, another famous television star, does needlepoint and considers it one of her favorite hobbies.

Both the Duke and the Duchess of Windsor do needlepoint. The King of Sweden made some very beautiful pieces. Many Hollywood stars work at needlepoint on the set while they are waiting. They find it is restful and they enjoy doing it. Many stars have beautiful Vertès pieces in their homes.

You don't need to be a Helen Hayes or Mary Martin or Betty Furness to get pleasure and profit out of this very interesting work.

The Dowager Queen Mother Mary, the good and distinguished queen of England, spent many hours during the last eight years of her life making the magnificent rug which we so proudly display on opposite page. This rug was auctioned off and brought over $100,000 for a favorite charity. The buyer very generously gave the rug to a museum. It is beautiful in color, magnificent in workmanship, and it is really a treasure in needlepoint.

Wide World Photos, Inc.

COME IN THE EVENING
OR COME IN THE MORNING
COME WHEN YOU'RE LOOKED FOR
OR COME WITHOUT WARNING

Developing Family Records in Needlepoint

MANY FAMILIES have had the important milestones of life recorded in needlepoint. A good alphabet and figures 1 to 10 are necessary. You can buy graph paper (square rules) at your stationer. Get the one-tenth-inch size. Buy it in sheets or tablet. The paper should be long enough for a row of letters giving the Christian name, such as "Audrey Arnold."

Take a piece of square ruled paper. Block out the data. For example:

Joann Jankus—Born March 15, 1926
Married to Richard Greener, Sept. 15, 1951

Use name and dates you wish to record.

Decide the color you will use. Do not hesitate to use several colors, mixing them in as you would in cross-stitch.

You can make the letters and figures the size you want simply by following our guide patterns for form, counting the stitches on graph paper, blocking out the design you wish to transfer to canvas. Indicate first with pencil on your graph paper over the lines, counting each square as you go, so that all letters or numerals will be uniform in height and width and spacing. You can use colored crayons to indicate where you want colors on your design. Put this color in with the point of the pencil in the squares of your graph paper design.

After your wording is complete on the paper, find the exact center of your canvas by folding it in four. Place a pin at the exact center. (Pull sewing thread through as a marker.)

Be sure when beginning to mark your canvas that you place your words or numbers so that you do not have to crowd as you approach the right-hand side in your marking. Have uniform space between letters and figures, so they are readily readable. To insure this, count the number of rows of lettering you will have, measure the height of the letters and how much space between the rows needed to separate them for good affect. Count the meshes on your canvas, up from center, so that you will know where the top of the first row of lettering is to begin. Count the number of letters on each side of center. Start working on first row of letters on extreme left side and proceed down canvas, row after row, until wording is completed. See diagram **A**.

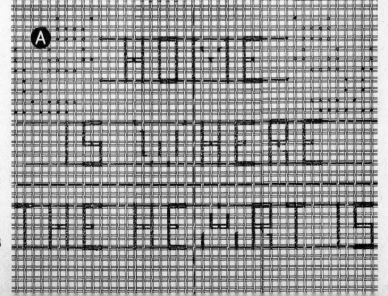

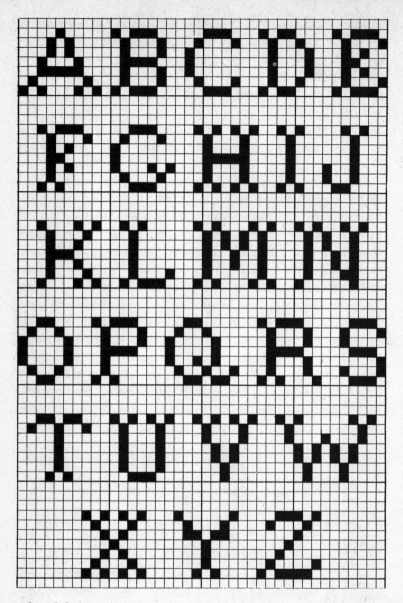

The alphabet above can be used on any size canvas and the letters picked out to spell any word desired. For very small letters such as used in indicating the initials and date on a piece of needlepoint, use the letter to guide you for the shape and make with the petit point stitch.

The numerals can be used in the same way as the alphabet. Try to make it a rule always to initial and date your needlepoint, inconspicuously. It will be interesting to you and to those fortunate enough to inherit such pieces. The border shows what can be done in filling in a border with needlepoint stitches.

Making Your Own Designs

DECIDE WHAT YOU WANT. Buy a colored picture or greeting or post card, or card from a museum. Buy yarns to match the colors and then set about sketching in with pencil on your graph paper the design you want. It is a good idea to pin or preferably to baste your copy picture to a corner of the canvas so it is always before you to help you in proportioning the colors.

If you wish to make a copy of a bouquet or something from a still life, painting or drawing, block it out on your graph paper,

simplifying as much as possible. Color your graph paper to best carry out the colors of the design you have chosen. Then keep this before you as you work.

When the design is marked as desired on your graph paper, find exact center of your canvas by folding it in four. Place a pin at exact center (pull sewing thread through as marker).

Now, work up and down and to the two sides from center, so your design when worked out is properly centered on your canvas. You will be delighted with the way the design drops into place.

You can get ideas for designs from anything that appeals to you and that you feel you would like to copy—a bird on a limb,

a dog with a child, a flower from your garden. The graph paper will enable you to make an attractive design. Then, you meticulously put your stitches permanently on canvas to produce your own original design.

Try doing a silhouette of your own home—the outline of trees, a gate, a trellis, a boy on a bicycle, or some event important to you.

Mrs. Theodore Roosevelt, Jr., designed and made many pieces, mostly of museum exhibition quality. These depicted scenes from her husband's active life, also events that concerned her and her children. Many magazine and newspaper stories have been written about these masterpieces. No doubt pictures of these can be

seen in your public library. If you are interested in developing personalized needlepoint designs, seeing Mrs. Roosevelt's might prove helpful.

Geometric Borders and Pictures. Many people like to take plain canvas and express their own ideas. This is easy enough to do. Lay the design out carefully on graph paper with a ruler and pencil, making all your marks true. Count carefully so your finished work will be even. The beautiful pictures on the two preceding pages show how individual ideas can be developed to make an attractive whole.

Floral with a Border. The border is blocked out on the graph paper with pencil. Count carefully so when working the canvas your work will be even. A yarn color to match the most prominent flower is used for the border. The piece is made with the simplified half-cross stitch.

Needlepoint as a Hobby

NEEDLEPOINT AS A HOBBY appeals to many. Individuals have become authorities on stitches, then tapestries, then early needlepoint designs. Needlepoint is an absorbing study because it began really as tapestry. The superb pieces in the Cloisters in New York City attest to the interest in this art that is centuries old. A tapestry tells a story and so can a piece of needlepoint.

Some collect only Victorian needlepoint pieces. Others concentrate on designs having only lilies in their collection. Mottoes are collected by many. Others select hunting scenes; still others, religious subjects. Some make a hobby of scenes from their own homes. To tell all about needlepoint would take many volumes. We hope the "how to" in this book will arouse your interest to the extent that you will follow the facet that appeals to you and find a beneficial and gratifying hobby as a result.

Color

COLOR TALKS. It has a language known the world around. Needlepoint in color is understood and appreciated by all peoples.

In Queen Victoria's bereavement, she made black a fashion, and for decades black was thought the proper background for needlepoint. Not so today. Home furnishings in the modern vein have brought light colors to the fore. Off-white and palest beige or palest blue are favorites. Off-white background for needlepoint, with clear scintillating colors in the design, is exciting to work and practical to use because one need never worry about needlepoint soiling. The fine quality of yarn used for needlepoint cleans readily with any reliable fabric cleaner.

Sometimes dark colors are preferred for accent—the deep reds, the lovely greens, the warm browns.

Along with the many shades of green that one can use, come the pale yellows and clear bright reds; also soft old rose or delicate pinks. Decorators like all these as accents, or to emphasize or subdue a color scheme.

A bride-to-be building her hope chest has but to dream of the color scheme in her home to begin to plan a set of covers for her dining room chairs, a needlepoint piece for a beautiful boudoir chair or a dressing table bench, or perhaps a card table cover with seats for a matching set of four chairs.

Decorators insist that the colors in rooms adjacent to each other should have an integrated link that makes them kin. For example, if the walls of one room are green, then the carpet of the room that leads to it could be green. If the draperies are ivory, then the needlepoint backround of a pair of chairs, pillows for a couch, or the center inside a scroll design of a set of chairs could well be of ivory to harmonize with the draperies.

Colors for needlepoint background yarns are abundant and exquisite in tone, again because of the excellent quality wool of which they are made. Just the right colors for your purpose, for suitable matching or sharp contrast, should be easy to find.

Color and Period Furniture

IF YOU HAVE period furniture—French Provincial, Early American or modern, or any one of the different periods—visit museums and libraries. Study pictures of rooms that use the type of furniture you have. You will find such research rewarding and excitingly interesting. Sometimes you need to go where the photographs and prints are filed in order to get pictures of good rooms of the period in which you are interested, but do go—you will see from these just what goes with what to make a happy balance in a room.

It is said that the average woman has but one time in her life when she provides things for her home with deliberation. After she has acquired pieces of furniture, paintings and other essentials of a nice home, she has to live with these; and if she makes a mistake in the beginning, that mistake will haunt her always. So take care at the outset to avoid mistakes. If you are buying anything new, take special care that you do not make unfortunate purchases—they are all too common, and too often must be lived with.

Go to drapery departments and shops, wallpaper and paint stores. Get samples of colors that appeal to you. Work out a palette of colors for your room, or for each room you are decorating. Every good home decorator does this. She hunts and finds colors that go together, that harmonize or contrast as her need requires. Then she determines how much of each color she can use to get a good balance and make a room happy for her family to live in.

Needlepoint means color. Once you have decided your floor and wall color, let needlepoint colors give oomph and accent, or dignity to chairs, couches, pillows, wall hangings and accessories.

Remember, in buying a piece of needlepoint, to choose colors in your design and background yarn that will blend with the other colors in your room.

Use needlepoint with its great versatility of color to create a harmonious picture.

Your background yarn should always be lighter or darker in

color than the already worked outer edges of the design. In a floral, be particularly careful that the leaves or stems do not fade into the background. When using a rose background, for example, watch that the same rose color is not predominant in the design itself. Lay the skeins of yarn up close to the design and see the effect of the background color against the design so that when your work is finished, you will be pleased with it.

Be sure to select colors that have an affinity with you and yours. Choose colors that are adaptable to your type of color scheme. Needlepoint will last you for generations and far beyond your present fabric furnishings. When a change in furnishings is made —new draperies and rugs—you, of course, will want to use your needlepoint and have it fit in as beautifully as when it was new.

Needlepoint Colors for Your Home

FIRST, EXAMINE YOUR ROOM carefully to determine whether or not you require harmonizing or contrasting colors for the backgrounds.

If walls, draperies and rug are in the same family of color, then very probably your needlepoint should contrast.

If draperies and walls contrast with the rug, the needlepoint can harmonize or contrast with one or the other. Chairs, footstools, benches may be worked in related color to provide contrast in a room.

Dining room chairs can have four or six of one background color, with the armchairs of another color. This is often done so that the armchairs may be taken into the living room when extra chairs are needed.

Some like to have the designs on dining room chairs each different, but in harmony—the background color the same for each. Manufacturers make up sets in this way. Remember that floral patterns can be used on almost all period furniture; fruit is preferred by many for Early American.

Modern furniture can well use the floral or fruit motifs, or the repeat and over-all patterns. Modern takes either a light or dark background, depending upon the wood and the color scheme of the room.

Needlepoint by Machine

NEEDLEPOINT HAS BEEN DONE by the distaff side of Singer Sewing Machine Company, making beautiful chair seats, cushions and pictures on the machine. This is highly specialized work and one needs an instructor to guide one in learning how to fill in the background stitches by machine.

Some Needlepoint History

FROM THE TIME that man could make yarn and before looms were invented, tapestries told the story of nations. They invariably were designed to record events and fashions of their time.

Tapestry is woven by the worker, using many bobbins, each wound in a different color yarn. The tapestry grows in its two-warp frame or loom as the bobbins are twisted, turned, held, transposed from one position to another until the effect is achieved. The most intricate designs are worked out to perfection. Many times a worker has spent his entire working life on the creation of one great tapestry.

Surely tapestry can be called the mother of needlepoint because they have a certain relationship in materials, design, possibilities, appearance and purpose.

We who do needlepoint realize the convenience of canvas—the advantages to us of having the design worked ready for us to apply the background. Simple indeed, yet needlepoint gives us something to be proud of as the makers of great tapestries and owners of tapestries are proud.

Tapestry dates back to 3000 B.C., at which time it was made in Egypt, China, India and Persia. Examples of this early work may be seen in great museums—the Metropolitan Museum of Art or the Cloisters in New York, or the Boston Museum of Fine Art, for example.

The Greeks and Romans knew the art of needlepoint long before the French, yet France made a really great contribution to its development through the French canvas which we have mentioned elsewhere.

In the Middle Ages or Gothic era, tapestry was made by monks and used as decoration by churches and also for the all-important purpose of retaining heat.

Before central heating, layers of needlepoint tapestries were used in castles and churches as hangings to keep out drafts and as insulation against cold. These hangings served also as conversation pieces, as many times they had been created to record the history, events and fashions of the period. In the Gothic era, the scenes depicted were those of hunting, religion and royalty. During this time some needlepoint was made by court attendants, under the direction of the royal ladies.

In the Paris workshops, needlepoint was sponsored by Charles VI. During the occupation of Paris by the British in 1422, most of the craftsmen fled the country and the art lay dormant in France for over two hundred years.

During the Renaissance, Raphael and many of his contemporaries became interested in tapestry designing, and consequently the subject matter became a bit unrestrained as many of the existing pieces show.

In France the two Gobelin brothers, who originated the great Gobelin Tapestry Works (that are known round the world), settled where they are about 1597 because they were looking for a certain type of water to achieve the dyes they so wanted for

Below—Christmas Eve at Mount Vernon

their beautiful yarns. The Gobelins were experts in dyeing and became famous for their fourteen thousand different shades, particularly a glowing scarlet known the world over as Venetian red.

During this same period Aubusson tapestries were originated, again by two artists who had great skill, and who traveled the countryside restoring the damaged tapestries in various castles and churches. These men first settled in Felletin, later moving to Aubusson. The Flemish workers, with their great skill, added much to the beauty of the tapestries. A Flemish-made tapestry is highly prized today.

James I of England, in 1619, employed fifty craftsmen from Brussels to develop needlepoint tapestries. Van Dyck and Rembrandt inspired these men in their designs. The work also was good for England economically, as it utilized wool from the nation's sheep.

Napoleon was very sympathetic to the well-established Gobelins' factory—and helped the firm restore their magnificent works and encouraged the development of this art in every possible way.

In the nineteenth century (1865) the development of the French canvas, which continues to be so popular today, brought

The Cherry Pickers on opposite page

The Chess Players shown at right

to needlepoint a surge of enthusiasm. Practically every country took up the work with renewed zeal and developed designs appropriate to its nation and interests.

The Dowager Queen Mother Mary of England was one of the great enthusiasts of this beautiful craft and spent her spare time for eight years making a magnificent rug. See photograph page 113.

To develop your appreciation and your interest in this subject, a visit to the museum where tapestry and needlepoint—mother and child—are shown will develop an interest and an appreciation, not only of the techniques of needlepoint, but also of the magnificence of the designs.

Although tapestries were favored principally in Europe, each nation the world around has put its own stamp of approval on needlepoint, the outgrowth of tapestry. This was done by the creation in each nation of designs peculiar to itself. England, Italy, France, Austria, Sweden, Holland—each has its own preference in design, just as you yourself choose the type of design that you prefer for your house. Each country has developed its own special type of motif that made its needlepoint seem to belong definitely to that country, and an authority can usually tell on seeing a piece of century-old needlepoint in what country it was made.

Our finest designs of today come from colonies established in various countries where artists create the design and native women execute the exquisite stitches.

Needlepoint speaks a universal language. It is enjoyed and treasured by all nations. It could indeed be used for the making of a United Nations flag since it is known and treasured the world around.

Needlepoint as It Relates to Periods

IN THE DAYS OF CRUSADES, men, away for long periods of time, encouraged their women to copy portions of the large tapestries that adorned their walls—this because they had no other source of design. These patterns in the main consisted of large leaves with small castles, and were known as verdure patterns.

At that time, Cluny designs, copies of tapestries from the Cluny Museum in France, were favored. Needlepoint workers attempted to make stitches appear as nearly like the old tapestries as possible. This became a favorite period in needlepoint. The *"mille-fleurs,"* scattered animals and little stories were interesting as well as decorative. Fortunately they can be used on many periods of furniture, especially heavy woods. Because of color and design, such pieces are usually considered as museum or collectors' items. Such needlepoint is used chiefly for wall hangings.

Renaissance. Needlepoint designs of the Renaissance period—of the fifteenth century—continue in favor because of their rich designs and color. Deep, rich blues and reds showing Italian influence are outstanding. The "Horn of Plenty" is frequently used as part of the design. Background colors for such designs are often deep and dark, stained glass windows having influenced many designs both in form and color.

Louis XIV, the king of grandeur, reigning in the seventeenth century, had everything done on a tremendous scale—even to over-

BAROQUE
Louis XIV (1643-1715)

Golden Age; classic severity; compass curves. Curved ornaments; gilded; upholstered. Legs heavy, square, tapered, diagonal stretchers. Ebony; oak; walnut; chestnut; sycamore.

sized flowers in needlepoint designs. Furniture was massive in this baroque period, woods heavily carved and gilded.

Needlepoint or tapestry was a necessity for upholstery. Louis XIV encouraged the art of embroidery to the extent of having an embroidery factory established next to the famous Gobelin Works where he employed thousands of embroiderers.

FRENCH REGENCY (1715-1723)

Introduction of the free curve and use of cabriole leg and carved deer's hoof; curved stretchers.

Louis XV. As only royalty could support the art of tapestry weaving, most factories were run under the favor of kings. During this monarch's reign and the period of Madame de Pompadour, rococo was at its height. Scrolls, shells and spot placement of designs were favored. Gods and goddesses dressed in eighteenth century costume were depicted in needlepoint designs also—pastoral and Oriental scenes. Many designs of this period are of the wreath type with a two-color background—i.e., ivory in the center and pastels outside the design motif.

Furniture of the Louis XV period was covered with needlepoint reproductions, done in miniature, and copied from the famous wall tapestries of the Louis XIV period.

ROCOCO (1723-1774)
Louis XV (1715-1774)

Free curved line in structure and ornament. Cabriole leg; scroll foot. Smaller dimensions; delicate lines; upholstered.

An Oriental feeling was seen in Louis XV designs, this possibly because of Madame de Pompadour's financial interests in trade with China.

Louis XVI. Designs of this period are highly favored. In these one sees reflected the taste of both Madame de Pompadour and Marie Antoinette. The designs in the main are simple, with a marked tendency to daintiness. They are usually made with flowers and ribbons in soft pastels with darker pastel backgrounds, with centers in ivory.

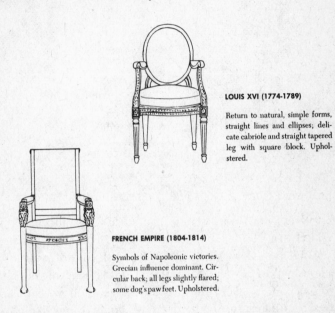

LOUIS XVI (1774-1789)

Return to natural, simple forms, straight lines and ellipses; delicate cabriole and straight tapered leg with square block. Upholstered.

FRENCH EMPIRE (1804-1814)

Symbols of Napoleonic victories. Grecian influence dominant. Circular back; all legs slightly flared; some dog's paw feet. Upholstered.

Directoire Period (1795 to 1804). This, the forerunner of the severe Empire period, is almost modern in feeling. We find a very noticeable change in design from lovely flowers and nosegays to severe classic forms. Decorations formerly favored by royalty were taboo. A jury of artists and manufacturers decided what would be made.

Empire Period. When Napoleon became Emperor of France, he commanded a new type of furniture known as Empire. It was a far cry from typical French furnishings. Because of campaigns in Rome and Egypt, we find the reflection of these countries and

Napoleon's conquests everywhere—lyres, laurel wreaths, swords, winged human figures, Napoleon's "Star of Destiny" as well as his initial, the familiar "N" surrounded by a laurel wreath. All these were interpreted as designs for fabrics, tapestries and needlepoint. Empire furniture in its original design is too formal and sometimes too ponderous for the ordinary home. However, there are simpler forms in modern adaptations which are enjoyed by many.

TUDOR (1509-1603)
HENRY VIII, ELIZABETH

Gothic forms dominated. Gradually influenced by Italian Renaissance. Age of oak furniture commenced. Wainscot chair; waxed; square leg.

Tudor. Needlepoint was highly favored in England during the reign of Henry VIII in the sixteenth century. This art was brought to England by Henry VIII's first wife, Catherine of Aragon, an accomplished needlewoman. Educated in the convents of Spain, she brought to England the needlework skills. It was she who made soft cushions for the hard, heavy, crude, thronelike chairs. She also embroidered small medallions, often coats-of-arms or heraldic shields, and appliquéd them to cushions and chair-back panels.

Gradually, through Catherine's efforts, needlepoint designs became distinctly English. The Tudor rose, thistle, sprig patterns and heraldry designs were worked in bright, natural colors, with background colors somber.

Elizabethan. By the time Elizabeth became queen, living in England had greatly advanced. The steel needle was introduced, and England gets the credit for it. Fishbones and thorns were used previously. After the steel needle, fine stitches became easier to make and consequently more delicate effects obtained. Elizabeth herself was as able a needlewoman as Catherine of Aragon, and urged the ladies of her court to make embroideries and held frequent contests within the court to inspire beautiful work.

Printing became popular during this period, and we find exquisite petit point designs on book covers. As few could read or write, the design on the cover told a story. People read the picture rather than the text. For some reason, this period gives us designs of insects, bugs, bees, butterflies. One piece of needlepoint shows different scenes, disconnected thoughts, all with the one object of telling a story.

During this period, Mary Queen of Scots—also an accomplished needlewoman—learned the art of embroidery in the French court from her mother-in-law, Catherine de Medici. Museums in England today show excellent examples of Mary Queen of Scots' needlepoint.

JACOBEAN (1603-1660)
JAMES I, CHARLES I, CROMWELL

Gothic elements supplanted by accurate Renaissance forms. Last ten years saw religious wars and industrial, artistic stagnation. High paneled back; oak; waxed; turned or twisted leg.

Jacobean (1603 to 1649). These designs, usually a mass of flowers and foliage and stump work, came into fashion about 1603 during the reign of England's King James I. Jacobean designs were brilliant and background colors somber to contrast and to accentuate the design itself.

William and Mary brought to England from Holland a definite color change. England was trading with China; therefore Oriental type designs became popular, needlepoint upholstery reflecting the strong colors of the highly favored imported Oriental fabrics.

Lifelike masses of flowers were now being used in needlepoint designs. Mary, an ardent needlewoman, had practically every bench and chair in the castle covered with needlepoint. A bishop said of her needlepoint, "She works with a diligence as though to earn her bread by it." The same earthy colors used for Jacobean colorings continued in favor with William and Mary pieces.

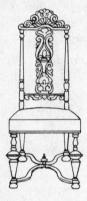

WILLIAM and MARY (1689-1702)

Age of walnut commenced. Simplicity. Wood graining and marquetry. Legs turned with mushroom, bell and inverted cup forms; bun feet; polished.

Queen Anne. Her reign was short but influential, especially in furniture design. Her period is credited with making the first furniture in England that was both good to look at and comfortable to sit on.

The cockleshell is frequently used as decoration on a Queen Anne chair. Hunting scenes, especially Oriental ones, are typically Queen Anne.

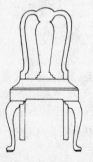

QUEEN ANNE (1702-1714)

Introduction of curved line, Chinese forms and lacquer. First use of mahogany. Spoon back; splat; walnut; polished; cabriole leg; club or pad foot.

More furniture of this period is in museums and private collections today, having needlepoint coverings, than of any other period. Fire screens bespeak this period, as every house of the eighteenth century had a fireplace, with a decorative screen in front of it.

EARLY GEORGIAN (1714-1750)

Decorated Queen Anne. Heavier structure; natural graining; exclusively mahogany after 1733. Increased carving; paw and ball foot.

Georgian Period. This pertains to the reign of the four Georges. During this time Chippendale, Hepplewhite, Sheraton, and the Adam brothers designed and made fine furniture. After Queen Anne, the names of the periods actually change from kings and queens to the leading cabinetmakers. All these periods are popular today and some houses are furnished with a mixture of all four.

Chippendale. This period gives us three types of designs—Gothic Chippendale, Chinese Chippendale and Chippendale. Needlepoint background colors in this period were usually dark. Usually a Chippendale chair has a slip seat, ideal for placing needlepoint.

MIDDLE GEORGIAN (1750-1770)
CHIPPENDALE (1718-1779)

Designs ranged from extreme rococo to classical severity. Elaborated splat back; ribband; ladder; wheat sheaf; Chinese forms. Mahogany polished. Cabriole leg. carved foot; straight leg, club foot.

Hepplewhite. Louis XVI furnishings, classically delicate, were the obvious inspiration for Hepplewhite. The "Three Feathers" of the Prince of Wales decorated many a design. Wheat ears, drapery, garlands of ribbons and festoons were also favored. The lines were delicate, conforming to the type of furniture.

ADAM (1728-1792)

Classic forms of Pompeii became standard of design. Delicacy of detail embellished it. Characteristic back is oval. Mahogany; gilt; turned leg

HEPPLEWHITE (1760-1786)

Age of satinwood. Surfaces enriched with painted motifs. Shield, camel, oval, heart, wheel backs; mahogany and satinwood; polished; slender leg; spade foot.

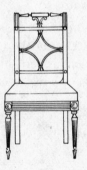

LATE GEORGIAN (1770-1810)
SHERATON (1750-1806)

The straight line predominated. Rectangular back; mahogany; satinwood; polished; turned and tapered leg; spade foot.

Sheraton. This craftsman gave us straight lines in contrast to the curves of Hepplewhite. Sheraton depended upon rare woods for the simplicity of his lovely chairs. Dainty floral motifs in needlepoint, often interlaced with crossbars, are favored for Sheraton chairs. See bench page 83.

Victorian. During this historic, and so recent period, needlepoint was favored as covering for chairs, and it seems everyone in England took it up. Many squared, or charted designs were used, which explains why women in moderate circumstances could do needlepoint at that time.

VICTORIAN (1837-1880)

Louis XV and Eastlake influence. Black walnut. Lack of refinement in form and detail.

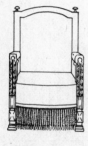

VICTORIAN (1837-1901)

All periods of the past and Mediterranean countries were sources of inspiration; Louis XV was strongest influence. Black walnut; mahogany; ebony; rosewood.

Fashion also favored all pieces in a room matching, so needlepoint became the occupation of entire families—all working to complete the coverings of all furniture in a favored room.

During this period black became important as a background when, upon the death of Prince Albert, Queen Victoria led the entire country in mourning him. Black horsehair covering also became fashionable. Previously black had not been used for upholstery. The deep, rich Burgundies, eggplants and blues can easily and much more happily be substituted for black with Victorian furnishings.

It is reported that Queen Victoria's first assignment in embroidery was a full-blown rose. She was partial to this and the large cabbage roses became popular in the Victorian era, and continue so for that type of furniture.

Early American Furniture. There is some furniture that is truly American, and not copies of actual furniture brought from Europe. The Hickok, for example, shown off to best advantage with fruit designs or small florals, is illustrated on page 16. Needlepoint on cherry and maple was often used with lined pads fitted to the seats of chairs or benches.

The Duncan Phyfe period, reflecting as it does the Empire period, is ideal for needlepoint. Floral medallions, sprays of flowers and geometric forms are favored.

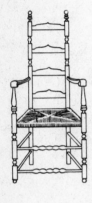

EARLY AMERICAN (1608-1720)
New England from 1660

Rectangular construction of Jacobean maintained. Oak, pine and orchard wood. Wainscot, slatback; mushroom finial — rush or board seats. Lambert Hitchcock was an important designer in this period.

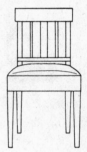

FEDERAL AMERICAN (1780-1830)

Influence of Adam, French Empire, English Regency. Classic forms and ornament.

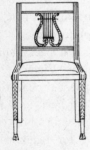

AMERICAN REGENCY
Duncan Phyfe (1784-1854)

Sheraton, French Empire influence. Graceful proportions. Grecian curve in chair backs and legs. Mahogany.

Biedermeier (1800 to 1850). This is a less severe German interpretation of French Empire period. Many decorators use it in modern settings. The seats are especially suitable for needlepoint. Shown at top of opposite page.

BIEDERMEIER (1800-1850)

Name from German cartoon character. Style, combination of French Empire and painted peasant work. Farm and orchard wood, some mahogany.

Modern. This type of design came into being prominently with the Paris Exhibition in 1925. The early American designs, especially the Shakers' gave us forerunners of stark simplicity in furniture. In 1910, the Mission furniture—ugly as it was—had a relationship to the first real modern. Bauhaus of Germany contributed further to the modern mode. Then came classic, then Swedish modern.

Modern today really means restrained, unembellished, without ornament. Textured fabrics, rugs, draperies and upholstery are favored with modern furniture. Needlepoint, being textured, fits in ideally. Flowers, geometrics and border designs all are ideal needlepoint designs for use with modern décor.

Previously, furniture had been adaptations of previous periods.

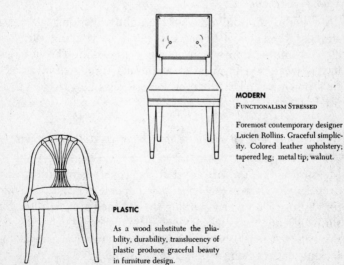

MODERN
FUNCTIONALISM STRESSED

Foremost contemporary designer Lucien Rollins. Graceful simplicity. Colored leather upholstery; tapered leg; metal tip; walnut.

PLASTIC

As a wood substitute the pliability, durability, translucency of plastic produce graceful beauty in furniture design.

To Help You with Needlepoint

You now know what needlepoint is.

The simplest form of hand embroidery, it is worked on canvas using a blunt needle and yarn or floss.

You now know that needlepoint gets crooked when you work.

There is no known reason except possibly the way we hold it when we work. This lopsidedness happens to most people when working, particularly with the continental stitch. When the work is completed, however, it is simple and ever so practical to block a piece straight.

You now know that you should not cut your yarn too long.

Yarn should be cut about eighteen or twenty-two inches long (see yarn cutting instructions). Long strands may twist and tangle and wear thin, giving inadequate coverage on the front of your canvas. Short strands are easily handled and retain a desirable fluffiness that fills in the meshes more evenly.

You now know why the canvas can show through in spots as you work your needlepoint.

This results from pulling wool too tightly, working with long strands, letting wool twist as working, or working yarn too close to the end on which needle is threaded. The last few inches wear thin from constant pulling through canvas and thus don't cover last three or four stitches as yarn length is used.

You now know how to measure an object to determine size of canvas needed.

Measure entire top of object to be covered, including any drop down side where finished needlepoint is visible. Provide for an extra inch when marking the outlined area to allow for shrinkage and ease when needlepoint is being mounted on the object. Usually two extra inches of unworked canvas for tacking under chair or object is desirable.

You now know why you should buy larger size canvas than you actually need.

Buy it, of course, if the design you want is on this canvas. You pay in the main for stitches in a design, and not for the size of the canvas. The cost is figured primarily on the number of stitches that have been worked. For example, the design may be an appropriate size for many objects and it would be disappointing if the canvas were not large enough to be used for your purposes. Consequently, twenty-six- or twenty-eight-inch canvases have designs in good proportion for average-size dining room chairs. Naturally, the larger the design, the less background wool needed and less work for you in completing the piece.

You now know how to determine the proper background color for your needlepoint.

You wouldn't pick a design with red predominating if the room it was to be used in were all soft red tones. Pick your design with your own color scheme or schemes-to-be in mind. Once you select the design, forget the colors in it and carefully choose your background yarn. The background color you select is all-important to your color scheme.

If you are making needlepoint as a gift with no idea as to what colors would be preferred, it is good to stick to neutral shades such as eggplant, ivory, gray or some shade of neutral green or softest rose—colors which pick up nature's colors and will tend to blend in almost any color scheme.

Black has long been a popular color, but it is hard on the eyes and unless specifically desired is not decoratively the most suitable color. There are about sixty needlepoint colors that have been developed by all manufacturers. From these you can choose just the right color for your home, whether period or modern.

You now know the type of wool to use for needlepoint.

One which is real needlepoint or tapestry wool, one which has been developed expressly to withstand fraying as it is drawn constantly through the canvas. It is made of long fibers, usually is mothproof, and its colors are resistant to light. Real needlepoint wool insures longer life in use and, of course, greater ease in working.

You now know that you need not work the entire canvas.

Place canvas on object to be covered. Mark off (with pencil) the entire area to be worked in needlepoint. Allow one extra inch on all sides to be worked to permit blocking, fit, etc. Make uneven basting stitches with thread over pencil line so area to be worked will remain clearly defined while you are working the piece.

You now know how tightly you should draw the stitches.

Using short strands, pull the needle through with one follow-through motion letting stitch set in place, neither too loosely, nor too tightly. Relax, and use an even pressure. Do this in a rhythmic way so that you have uniform work and enjoy making the stitches.

You now know what size needle to use and the kind essential to needlepoint.

There are blunt-end needles designed especially for needlepoint. For gros point—18 or 19 (18 usually preferred because larger eye makes it easier to thread it). For petit point—22 or 24.

You now know that needlepoint is suitable for all types of furniture.

The right design and background color which you select carefully will insure its suitability to your purpose.

You now know that needlepoint is not harder on the eyes than other handwork.

The regular ten-mesh canvas worked in the gros point stitch makes for very little eyestrain and in many cases stitches are made while watching television with no added weariness. There is no counting whatsoever and the large meshes are easy to see, alleviating any undue strain. All you need to see is where to put the needle in for each stitch. You don't need your eyes to pull the yarn through.

144

You now know that you need not buy all the colors to put in your design like those you see on the counters.

This is because the designs have already been worked for you by skilled needlepoint experts. The background is all that remains to be worked. There is no longer any need, unless original designs are your hobby, to have a large workbasket filled with hundreds of assorted yarns that have to be blended in various shadings—and it is no longer necessary to thread needles thousands of times to fill in different colors. All the time-consuming work is done for you.

You now know that the stitch which is worked across the canvas at an angle and keeps the canvas straight is the basket weave.

The basket weave stitch takes more yarn than the continental or the half-cross. Even so, many workers enjoy making this stitch.

You now know where to start working on your needlepoint.

For regular half-cross—start in upper left corner of outlined area and work from left to right. For the simplified half-cross —start in lower right corner and work vertically up length of canvas. For continental stitch—start from upper right corner of outlined area and work horizontally from right to left.

As you run out of wool, alternate places on the back of the piece where you end off, so that no ridges form on back or front. Use any excess yarn in your needle to fill in and around the design.

You now know that the continental stitch does not take twice as much wool as the half-cross.

It takes only one-quarter yard more to work one square inch of continental—one and a quarter yards for the continental stitch, and one yard to work one square inch in the half-cross.

You now know the difference between petit point and gros point and that both are needlepoint.

Petit point is the tiny stitch worked over every thread in the canvas including the ones locked together. Gros point is worked over two threads at all times. Needlepoint includes everything: Petit point, gros point, tramé, Bargello.

You now know what tramé is—not a finished picture.

Tramé means underlay (French). It is placing wool yarn on canvas to indicate proper colors to be worked to complete the picture. Instead of painting on canvas to indicate colors of design, tramé is placed in petit point meshes as a color guide. The colored yarn for working comes with all tramé pieces. Regular half-cross stitch beginning in the upper left-hand corner is worked over the wool underlay.

You now know how to block needlepoint.

See detailed instructions on page 64.

You now know whether to leave long ends of yarn on the wrong side.

Cut the ends of the yarn off to within one-eighth of an inch of the stitch. (Cut as you finish each needleful.)

You now know how to piece needlepoint.

See detailed instructions on page 67.

You now know how to determine quantity of yarn needed to fill in background with half-cross or continental stitches.

See details on page 12.

You now know how you can prevent yarn from twisting as you work.

Use short strands. Let the wool drop in natural position after working a stitch. Learn to roll the needle in your fingers so that the yarn is straight for every stitch and never twisted.

You now know why it is best to work one way on a canvas.

You do not lose time by trying to avoid catching the yarn as you come from underneath in a row. Also you avoid any possibility of ridges.

Index

74 75 76 77 10 9 8 7 6 5 4 3 2 1